FINDING A JOB AFTER 50

Reinvent Yourself
for the
21st Century

JEANNETTE WOODWARD

CAREER
PRESS
Franklin Lakes, NJ

FINDING A JOB AFTER 50
EDITED BY JODI BRANDON
TYPESET BY EILEEN DOW MUNSON
Cover design by Foster & Foster, Inc.
Printed in the U.S.A. by Book-mart Press

To order this title, please call toll-free 1-800-CAREER-1 (NJ and Canada: 201-848-0310) to order using VISA or MasterCard, or for further information on books from Career Press.

CAREER
PRESS

The Career Press, Inc., 3 Tice Road, PO Box 687,
Franklin Lakes, NJ 07417
www.careerpress.com

Library of Congress Cataloging-in-Publication Data

Woodward, Jeannette A.
    Finding a job after 50 : reinvent yourself for the 21st century / by Jeannette Woodward.
        p. cm.
    Includes index.
    ISBN-13: 978-1-56414-894-0
    ISBN-10: 1-56414-894-7
    1. Job hunting—Handbook, manuals, etc. 2. Middle-aged persons—Employment—Handbooks, manuals, etc. I. Title. II. Title: Finding a job after fifty.

HF5382.7.W68 2007
650.14084'6—dc22

2006016819

To the most important people in my life—

Chris,

Laura,

John,

and

Lowell.

Contents

Introduction

Bob is 61 and he has a new job. It pays peanuts, it's on the bottom rung of the career ladder, it comes with no power and few perks, but he couldn't be happier. He's doing what he loves to do. Bob found the job only after being turned down for a dozen similarly unimpressive openings. In fact, Bob probably put more time and effort into finding this job than any of the high-power, executive positions that fill his resume.

Shelley is 60 but she can't afford to take a job such as Bob's. A single mom, she has never been able to put aside the kind of nest egg she needs to retire comfortably. Helping with her kids' college tuition, paying down the mortgage, and maintaining a middle-class lifestyle have left her with too many debts to retire. Shelley knows she'll have to go on working, but does she really have to remain in the boring, emotionally draining job she's held for years? Is it too late to begin a new and more satisfying career?

It's a Jungle Out There

The job market is a scary place when you're 50 or 60; some have likened it to a combat zone. Battle-scarred veterans report that time after time, they're passed over for jobs that seem made for them. The successful applicants are half their age with only a fraction of their qualifications. So with a hefty retirement account, why did Bob endure the agony of the job hunt? Why should you be out there battling this boomer-unfriendly market if the prospect is so dismal? After all, maybe you could find a balmy beach somewhere and retire to a life of ease.

There was a time, not so very long ago, when people automatically retired at the age of 60 or 65, if they were fortunate enough to reach that ripe old age. Now many are still going strong, still passionately involved in their work at the age of 80. Why are they doing it? Why don't they just relax and take it easy? Many of the boomers and seniors who continue to work well past normal retirement age do so because they love their jobs. They get a lot of happiness from being with other people and they feel the deep satisfaction of doing something that really matters. If you are eagerly looking forward to retirement, you probably don't feel this sense of satisfaction. You may have become bored over the years and think of your job as nothing more than a daily grind, an endless succession of blue Mondays.

Maybe you've tried retirement, but found it's not what you expected. After years of going to work every day, you don't feel really comfortable out of the harness. But if you think back on your life before you retired, you realize you don't want to go back to that either. What do you really want to do with your life? Increasingly, baby boomers are answering this question by choosing new careers, ones that fit their particular strengths.

Who Are You?

None of us are quite the same people we were at 25. We've grown and we've developed different talents, skills, and interests; we finally know who we are and who we're not. We're no longer willing to let other people shape us into "company men" or "little women." If you're nearing the usual retirement age, you grew up in a very different world. Men were usually grateful to find a job on the bottom rung of the corporate ladder and advance gradually, remaining loyal to the same employers for much of their careers. Women didn't even think about careers. They were more likely to pick up a job when the children got older. They worked, not for personal gratification, but to pay for the kids' braces or otherwise supplement the family income.

You're Not Your Parents

Our parents came of age during the Great Depression and impressed on us the need for job security. They lived through times when they were really at the end of their ropes. Despite occasional recessions, those bad old days are gone. Most of us have had some pretty rough times, but we usually got back on our feet quickly. We can also expect to live longer than our parents. Although the numbers vary for different sexes and population groups, we can expect to live roughly 18 years after we reach age 65. With increased security and a longer life expectancy has come the realization that we want more out of life. We hope that we'll live to be a hundred, but those birthdays are piling up. If we really want to get the most out of the years ahead, we'd better get started immediately.

Rediscovering Your Dreams

So what is it that you really want? You may never have asked yourself that question before, especially when you were job-hunting. When you were young, your imagination wove dreams about what you would do when you grew up. However, the reality of the job market quickly won out over those dreams and the questions you began asking revolved around salary, advancement, and benefits. In all probability, those questions are no longer very relevant. Your children are grown and your other financial burdens are lighter. Social Security and Medicare will provide a safety net if not a comfortable income. Even keeping up with the Joneses no longer holds much appeal. What really matters is, in a word, happiness! Can you pause in the middle of a busy day and say, "I'm having a good time; I'm enjoying myself"? If the answer is usually *no*, do you have any idea what the sort of job might give you this sense of delight and contentment? Can you look back and recall such moments in the past?

Pulling Your Own Strings

Many people report that their best jobs were the ones in which they had control over their time and could pursue a project with some degree of independence. They look back on times when they felt creativity and innovation flowing through their veins. They felt stressed when they lost that freedom. What kinds of activities make you feel that your veins are pulsing with creativity? What do you do well and what kind of work gives you pleasure?

By now, you also know the things you are not good at. You know where you have encountered failure, and there's no longer any need to revisit those agonizing moments. Everyone has strengths and weaknesses. Now that you know yours, you can chart a course that capitalizes on your assets. Before you begin remembering all those things you did badly, however, consider that many of your personal qualities are neither positive nor negative in themselves. When you apply them to the wrong task, they can defeat you but in another situation, they might become strengths. Maybe you're a night owl who arrived late for important business meetings. If time after time, you felt guilty and inadequate, you probably never stopped to realize that there are many jobs that night owls do best.

Do You Feel Old and Out of Touch?

It is no longer possible to force employees to retire at a certain age. If you're in good health and your work is satisfactory, you can continue working indefinitely. But although they can't be forced to retire, many boomers report that they experience subtle pressure. They are made to feel as if they're old gaffers who are gradually excluded from the action. They are patronized by younger staff and made to feel like outsiders in their own offices. Gossip sessions go silent as they approach, and everyone seems to know more about what's going on than they do. In other words, they feel as if they've been put out to pasture, even though they're still on the job. Men may find that, even though they're earning good salaries and technically in decision-making positions, they're repeatedly overlooked. Women may go from one dead-end job to another, getting satisfaction from none of them.

If we are honest, we should admit that others are not entirely to blame. Over the years, we've become bored. We don't feel challenged and we tend to do the same things in the same way, year after year. In addition, we resent all the new technology and the whiz kids who think they know all about it. Who wouldn't resent being patronized by a 22-year-old who lectures us about the World Wide Web or the latest project management software?

Why Work?

Because we don't want to live this way, we grasp at retirement as soon as it is financially feasible. Yet, think of all the enjoyable experiences you lose when you leave the workplace. First and most important are the friendships with coworkers and the opportunities to meet new people. Lunch is a social occasion, whether we munch our sandwiches at a local restaurant or gathered around a communal table in the staff lounge. We are actually paid to enjoy new experiences: workshops, training sessions, and even trips to conferences in agreeable places.

There's another side to work, however. There's the pressure of having to do too much too fast, and the stress of competing with younger, more energetic ladder-climbers. The fear of failure and the need to survive political infighting can take away every ounce of pleasure. Do you really want to remain in this kind of world for the rest of your work life? Are you getting enough satisfaction from your job to make it worth spending most of your waking hours either working or thinking about work?

How Do You Spend Your Time?

Although most of the stereotypes about aging are unfounded, it's true that as we get older we have less energy. If the same amount of energy is devoted to a job, then there's less for everything else. Some people find it helpful to ratchet down their work involvement a notch or two. Maybe this means a job where you don't take home a stuffed briefcase every night or spend hours stuck in rush-hour traffic. Maybe it means finding a part-time job that leaves more hours for leisure.

Whatever your own decision, it may mean a job change or even a radical change in your career track. As you can well imagine, it's not usually a wise move to go to your boss and ask for a less-stressful job. In fact, if you're struggling to prove that you're not over the hill, such a request might only serve as confirmation that your useful work life is over. Remember: You're seeking a more interesting, more rewarding experience. Being relegated to a mindless job with an office next to the broom closet is not what you have in mind.

If you really want a change, you may have to find a new employer and possibly a completely new career. Be warned, however, that this will be much more difficult now than it was when you were 25. You will have to equip yourself with the right tools and even the right weapons to succeed in today's job market. You will have to convince a younger boss, who unconsciously looks on you as an old fogy, that you are just the man or woman for the job.

It's a Jungle Out There

I think of this book as a "guerilla guide," and that's really no exaggeration. Getting the job you want will be a struggle and you will have to approach it as such. Your arsenal must be well stocked before you enter the fray, and you must know what you're up against. Even occasional subterfuge may be necessary to combat the stereotypes and misinformation that abound in the work environment.

Have you sent out your resume lately, or been to a job interview? Other baby boomers report that, again and again, they are passed over, even when they appear to be the best-qualified applicants. It is easy to jump to the conclusion that this is age discrimination, but the real answer is not that easy. Yes, it is true that employers may have negative and unfair stereotypes of older workers. They may believe that they are not as sharp or capable as younger employees, or will use more sick leave (not true). They may feel uncomfortable supervising people old enough to be their fathers or mothers, just as you may feel uncomfortable being supervised by someone young enough to be your own offspring.

What may be more important, however, is that supervisors tend to look for people similar to themselves. They imagine how they would do the job and then assume that that is the way the job should be done. They can talk and work more easily with the people who are most similar to them, who think the same way, who come from the same kind of background. If you look back on the times when you were doing the hiring, or even choosing a real estate agent or lawyer, you probably did the same thing. It may be a good thing to put your feet into someone else's moccasins, but it is very hard to do.

The Right Resume for the Wrong Job

If you look closer at baby boomers who are not coping well with today's job market, you will see some other common problems. For one thing, they have amassed outstanding resumes for the wrong job. Their resumes make them appear to be poised for the next rung on the job ladder they chose 20 or 30 years ago. Alarm bells ring when the natural direction of your resume does not correspond to the job you're applying for. What's wrong with you? Why are you willing to take a position with lower pay or in a different field? Another boomer would understand, but younger employers can't imagine themselves doing the same thing. They would not take such a job unless they had to, or unless their job security was in jeopardy. It doesn't add up, so they assume there must be something wrong with you. You must have a problem.

Once again, think back; imagine what you might have thought of such a strange resume. Wouldn't you wonder if such applicants have been asked to resign? Things couldn't be going well, or why else would they be willing to take what amounts to a demotion? The resume employers look for is one that shows gradual progress toward this particular job open-ing. Your resume probably screams that you don't fit the model. Later in this book, we'll take a closer look at that resume and see what can be done to turn off those alarm bells.

Did You Change Your Mind?

Maybe you aren't currently employed. One day, last year or last month, you decided that life was too short to spend your time working at a job you didn't enjoy. You decided it was time to retire or at least to take a breather before you re-entered the work world. Unfortunately, in this fiercely competitive job market, being unemployed is equivalent to the kiss of death. Employers are used to dealing with younger applicants and, again, they imagine themselves in similar cir-cumstances. People in mid-career do not quit their jobs with-out having another one firmly in hand. Look at your own resume. One job follows another, usually without a break.

What all this means is that, to be successful, you're go-ing to have to appear closer to the employer's image of the successful applicant. To be successful, you will need to adapt your credentials to meet employers' expectations, while at the same time convincing them that you have talents they won't find in a younger person. Because of your extensive experience, you have more to bring to a job. Once you learn to market yourself, you can pick and choose, selecting your experiences and skills that are especially well suited to a particular opening.

Remember, though, that you're choosing this job; it's not choosing you. You're hard to please, too, and, while employ-ers are looking you over, you're looking them over just as critically. Choose carefully. No matter what it pays, this is going to be the best job you've ever had.

So that's really what this book is all about. You are very likely the best man or woman for the job, but you're going to have to prove it. To do so, you must know what you're up against and how to beat it. Here we go. Consider this a basic training course in guerilla job-hunting.

1 Discovering What You Really Want Out of Life

Because we've begun by comparing the job hunt to guerilla warfare, let's continue with the same analogy. Before you leap into the fray, it is necessary to reconnoiter, or as the dictionary defines it, look around and make a preliminary inspection of the territory. In this case, the unknown and sometimes-hostile territory to be explored is the job market. Perhaps it would be a good idea to begin by asking yourself why you are interested in exploring the job market in the first place.

It is likely that, if you are in your 50s or 60s, you've been in your present job for a long time. One of our characteristics as older employees is that we stay put and do not hop from job to job. We have settled into our positions and statistics indicate that we are apt to remain with the same employer until retirement. Recent corporate downsizing has interfered with this pattern, and a number of people have found themselves in the job market when they had no desire to be there. However, it's still quite likely that you're doing more or less the same job that you have been doing for a good many years.

Are You Stuck in a Rut?

Sometimes, we remain in a job we dislike because we might lose our retirement pensions. Fortunately, recent legislation and retirement investment accounts are making it possible for people to take their nest eggs with them. If you're reluctant to change jobs for this reason, be sure you look carefully into your options. You may be worrying unnecessarily.

Talk with both your workplace HR rep and with a certified financial planner. Between the two of them, you should be able to get a clear enough picture of your financial situation to make an informed decision.

Even if pension loss is not the issue, you may still be reluctant to change jobs. You may allow years to pass while you complain bitterly. Yet somehow, you never get around to doing anything to make yourself happier or more productive. Some people let their miseries and frustrations go on too long; then they finally boil over. They wake up one morning and decide they've had it. They can't go on any longer and so they resign or retire without really considering how the decision will impact the rest of their lives.

Take a Reading

How do you really feel about your job? Sure, everyone complains, but do you really dislike going to work? Do you spend the weekend dreading Monday? Find a time to have a heart-to-heart talk with yourself when nothing out of the ordinary has happened at work, when you're not feeling particularly distressed or angry. Use this opportunity to go over the pluses and minuses of remaining in your present job. Take out paper and pencil and write down each response so you can see both sides clearly. Here are some basic questions to get you started:

➻ **How do you get along with your boss?**

Of course, we are all critical of the boss as a matter of principle. We can all be Dilberts, taking pleasure in catching the boss in foolish mistakes. However, some of us have more serious problems. Maybe your boss makes you feel inadequate. He or she does not tolerate mistakes, and so you live in fear that your failures will be discovered. Does your boss respect you or merely tolerate you? Ask yourself whether your relationship is just mildly irritating or interfering with your happiness and sense of well-being.

➻ **How do you get along with your coworkers?**

Interpersonal friction and rivalry are a natural part of the work experience, but sometimes it gets out of hand. When you think about the people you work with, the pleasure you get from their company should outweigh the negative side. Sure, there's always competition. There will be times when you resent their successes or feel angry that a decision was made behind your back. But if you don't feel happy to see at least some of your coworkers on Monday morning, then these hostilities have gone too far. Your work environment may be so highly competitive that you can never relax and enjoy one another. Sometimes, you can simply refuse to play that game and deliberately set about reestablishing relationships. Sometimes, however, that just isn't possible.

- **Is there a good balance between your personal life and your work life?**

  Do you have the time and the energy to do at least some enjoyable things during the week, or do you come home from work feeling so exhausted that you can do nothing more than collapse in front of the television? Of course, everyone's worn out after a long day at work, but does it feel as if your whole life is spent going to or recovering from work? Do you bring a pile of paperwork home with you? When your friend or spouse suggests dinner at a nice restaurant, does it seem to be too much of an effort? It's true that all of us occasionally need to take off our shoes and curl up for a nice quiet evening, but if this is what you do night after night, you have a more serious problem. Ask yourself what you really want to change and what you want to hold onto. If flagging energy is your main problem, maybe you can cut back a bit. Remaining in the same field as an independent consultant might be a better option.

- **Does your work involve travel?**

  If so, has it become increasingly stressful? Has the fun gone out of it? Does a business trip now mean little more than jetlag, a lonely hotel, and a cramped airline seat? As we get older, we tend to appreciate our own bed, our own bathroom, and our own routines a lot more than we did when we were young. With less energy at our disposal, we may not take advantage of the cultural and recreational opportunities that business travel offers. Are there ways that you can reduce travel with more phone calls and e-mail messages, or would this be viewed as failing to do your job?

How important are power and prestige to you?

Do you derive a sense of importance from your work? Do you get a lot of satisfaction out of being a leader who is looked up to by others in your company? In other words, is your job essential to your self-esteem? If you answered *yes* to these questions, you are not a good candidate for retirement, and a more relaxing, less stressful job may not satisfy your needs.

On the other hand, it may be time to take yourself in hand and examine your power and status needs. One of the people you will meet in the next chapter is Mel, a "captain of industry," who wheeled and dealed himself all the way to the top corporate echelon. Until he found his own way, Mel's later years were filled with anger at colleagues who shoved him aside, rejection by his family who refused to be treated as underlings, and frustration when power and prestige did not bring happiness. These are fleeting riches and there's always someone coming along behind you who will be delighted to take your place. Most people find that it is better to voluntarily surrender this corporate booty and seek a more satisfying lifestyle.

Does your job seem meaningless?

Do you feel as if your life hasn't gone in the direction you intended? When you were young, you probably wanted to save the world or at least make it a better place. As you became involved in your career, you tended to lose sight of those idealistic goals but they remained in the background, buried somewhere in the depths of your conscience. As you grow older, you may find yourself asking, "Why am I doing this? What does my life mean?" Does it seem that you've accomplished too little of real importance? Does the money you've earned seem less important than the values you've compromised? Everyone arriving at middle age must make peace with youthful dreams, but if this sense of dissatisfaction is eating away at you, now may be the time to do something about it. If you really want to make the world a better place, then do it!

↠ What would you do if you retired tomorrow?

Are rest and relaxation the first things that come to mind? Snoozing in your recliner will quickly lose its charm when you retire. Do you have hobbies and interests that you would pursue more actively in retirement, or do you merely have some vague ideas about leisure pursuits that interest you? If you don't have a definite plan filled with activities you already enjoy, then you're probably not ready for retirement. Once again, we human beings need to be actively involved in life. Retirement should represent a transition to a more enjoyable but still active lifestyle.

↠ How do you feel about a part-time job?

Many of us decide that part-time work is a good compromise between an all-consuming full-time job and no job at all. It can be a great choice, providing the pleasures that come with it outweigh the hassle. Part-time work can bring structure to your life when you might otherwise be feeling adrift and purposeless. Because the transition from a life centering around a job to a life without that center can be difficult, a part-time job allows you to make adjustments gradually, enjoying the best of both worlds.

Whether or not you remain with your present employer or look elsewhere, part-time jobs are often poor-paying, and part-timers may have little status. Benefits such as health insurance may be available only for full-time staff. Look into employers who encourage job-sharing, as this option can provide many of the perks of a full-time job without all those hours. Find out about the various ways you can obtain health insurance through local clubs and other organizations. For example, find out if your local chamber of commerce offers a policy to its members, and check into professional groups that attract self-employed businesspeople. If you will qualify for Medicare in just a few years, it may be worthwhile paying a somewhat higher premium to "buy" your freedom.

↠ If you're a woman, do you feel as if you never got your turn at bat?

Do you feel that you've never had the chance to do the things you imagined when you were growing up? Somehow a home and children absorbed your life and the dream of becoming a doctor, lawyer, or corporate executive was relegated to a back closet. Husbands and wives of the same age often find themselves at different stages in their personal development. Men may have spent their adult lives climbing the ladder of success, only to find that it never provided the satisfaction they were looking for. Women, on the other hand, may feel deprived. Through the years, they harbored dreams of exciting careers but subordinated those ambitions to the needs of their families. Now their children are grown and there is little reason why they should not, to paraphrase the inspiring Joseph Campbell, follow their bliss.

⥤ Do you want a new job or a whole new career?

How much time and effort do you want to put into your plan? Have you had an exhausting career and are looking for a job that will be less stressful? Do you want more leisure, or do you really want a career to which you can give your all? You will soon be meeting a woman who decided at the age of 60 to totally change both her personal life and her work life. She chose a profession that required several years in the classroom and an apprenticeship as well. This certainly meant giving her all, but, because she enjoyed preparing for her career just as much as her work as a professional architect, it was a good decision. Friends wondered why she wanted to embark on such a big goal so late in life. After all, she would have little time left to practice her profession. As it turned out, she is still going strong at the age of 90 and can look back on many happy and satisfying years.

⥤ Do you enjoy your present job and just want more time for yourself?

You might want to look into the prospects for independent contractors in your field or even in your own company. Independent contractors perform a variety of jobs but they work for themselves, not for an employer. They contract to perform certain work in their own way on their own schedule. Of course, their customers have some say in the matter but, in general, an independent contractor enjoys much more freedom than a full-time employee.

The downside of being a contractor is the loss of job security, including fringe benefits. Independent contractors are also burdened with much of the same paperwork and reporting requirements as other small businesses. However, they can control their workload by accepting or rejecting offers.

✎ Are you willing to go back to school?

This might mean a few computer courses just to brush up your skills, or it could mean a multi-year commitment. Do you enjoy learning new things? Does the idea of returning to the classroom sound like fun or just more work? To learn how it would really be to return to the classroom, you might want to take a course at your local community college. Take one of the more demanding classes that requires work. Be sure, however, to pick a subject in which you are interested. That way you will experience both the hard work and the rewards.

✎ Do you have the skills and temperament to start your own home business?

Computers and related technology have made it possible to run a successful business with very little financial outlay. It's usually a lot of hard work but, if it's work you enjoy doing, it may be the right choice for you. Do you like to make your own decisions and set your own schedule? Are you at your best when you are deep in a project and scarcely aware of the clock ticking?

✎ How's your motivation?

Both starting a home business and becoming an independent contractor require a lot of self-motivation. Is this one of your strengths? When you have a project to accomplish, do you approach it with enthusiasm, or are you a procrastinator? If you need the discipline imposed by deadlines or a boss telling you what to do, maybe you're not suited for this kind of life.

•◦ How would a job change or retirement affect your family?

Are your children on their own or still in need of financial assistance? What about your spouse? In a sense, whatever you do will be done together. Spend some time together talking about your dreams. Will you both retire or make a job change? Will you relocate? As I mentioned, men and women may be at different places in their lives. It might be a good idea for you both to write out your answers to these questions independently, then get together to discuss them. You don't need to agree, but you will certainly need to coordinate your work and leisure lives. Then you'll be in a better position to develop a plan that meets both of your needs.

You can probably think of other issues that will enter into any decision you make. As you jot down answers to these questions, you'll probably see patterns emerging. Some options are clearly more appealing than others.

Other Considerations

Most of us have frequently heard the axiom "stress will kill you!" and we may have used those same words when talking to friends. Medical science has determined that some people actually thrive on stress, and you may be one of these people. They enjoy confronting challenges every day and are actually having fun when their adrenalin is skyrocketing. For people who fit into this category, the sky's the limit as far as new work experiences are concerned. They can continue to work their way up their present career ladder or they can choose a different career and savor the challenges of struggling toward the higher rungs. They may, however, need to adjust their enthusiasms to their energy levels.

Unfortunately, however, most people don't fit into this category. Instead, our blood pressure rises when we find ourselves in a stressful work situation. We lie awake at night worrying, and our bodies take a lot of unnecessary punishment. For most people, stress can lead to a wide variety of illnesses including heart attacks at the age of 50. As you can readily understand, it is essential to know which category you fit into. It's also important to understand yourself as you are now, not as you were 20 or 30 years ago. We all change over the years, and our ability to cope with stress tends to decline.

Many of the previous questions will help with your personal diagnosis. However, the answer is not always so clearcut. You may enjoy some aspects of your job and you may still occasionally experience a "high" when you overcome a difficult problem. Did the questions make you aware that you no longer enjoy travel the way you used to or that your personal life has suffered because of the demands of your job? Do you now find that interpersonal conflicts bother you more than they used to? It's well worth spending some time thinking about the stressful aspects of your life. What you may have looked on as unavoidable irritations when you were younger may now threaten your health and future happiness.

Exploring Your Options

Once you've done some real soul-searching, make a list of all your options. You'll probably be surprised at how many there are. We tend to get into ruts and forget that we usually have many choices. The possibilities include:

- Remaining in your present job.
- Phasing in retirement by gradually reducing the number of hours you work each week.
- Retiring with an assortment of hobbies and volunteer activities to keep you busy and involved with other people.
- Finding a part-time job, either with your present employer or in a new organization.
- Becoming an independent contractor for your present employer or for several organizations.
- Going back to the classroom to learn new skills.
- Choosing and launching a new career.
- Starting a home business or other small business.

Add any others that you've been considering. Then, once you've made your list, cross out the ones that totally lack appeal. This should reduce the choices but still leave you with several viable options. Now list the positives and the negatives of each choice remaining on your list. Remember that you're not making the kind of decision you made when you were 25. Your life has been filled with many different kinds of experiences. You know yourself better and you're in a much better position to make a choice than that young innocent of the past. Ask yourself how each choice would suit you. That means resetting your mental clock to experiences you enjoyed years ago. What did you find difficult or boring?

Be Honest About Failures

As human beings, we have the bad habit of ignoring past lessons, and we often fail to learn from our mistakes. What's usually referred to as a "gut feeling" can sometimes tell us about our real needs but it can also keep sending us in the same unproductive direction again and again. Try to confirm your "gut feelings" with real experiences. Look back on times when you followed your instincts. Did it turn out to be a good idea? If your feelings are leading you in one direction, have you gone that way before and later been sorry?

None of us likes to remember our failures, but being honest now may lead to future successes. Everyone fails occasionally. Whether you managed to cover up your bad judgment, foolish mistakes, and ignorance, or whether your faults were held up to you by disgruntled bosses, failure brought humiliation and lowered your self-esteem. There are some things that no matter how hard you try, you will never be able to do well. If you examine your past, you will notice patterns and you will see yourself making the same mistakes over and over.

If on looking back, you see many failures, you were probably a square peg in a round hole. There was a poor match between your talents and the jobs you chose. If you see yourself as that square peg, then its time to be honest and move away from those round holes. Qualities that cause you to fail in one situation may help you succeed in another. Even though it may hurt to remember past miseries, try to analyze them. What was it about those jobs that brought out your weaknesses and how might things have been different? You don't have to relive the past. You have reached a wonderful point in your life when you can finally be yourself, so don't miss the opportunity.

Measuring Risk and Commitment

As you consider each of your options, try to estimate how much commitment is required. For example, opting for early retirement may mean a smaller pension and fewer benefits, so you'd better be sure this is what you really want to do. Such a choice requires a lot of commitment, because you probably can't get your job back if you decide that retirement is not for you. If you invest your life savings in a small business, you've also made a very large commitment. Selling out could be disastrous, so your whole future is resting on the choice. On the other hand, if a part-time job doesn't work out, you can probably find another.

Take a Good Look at Your Finances

So far, you have been focusing on what you want out of life because it is so easy to lose sight of your goals when you're facing the pressures of the real world. Nevertheless, you will need to come up with a practical plan that will allow you to pay your bills and meet your other responsibilities. How much money will you need? This is a question you may have trouble answering. Sometimes you assume that the amount of money you need is the amount you're currently earning. At other times, when your job seems particularly exasperating, you imagine that you could make do on a small fraction of your current income. The truth is somewhere between the two extremes. Some experts say that you should be able to count on 70 percent your current gross income. You'll never really know, however, until you make a real budget for yourself and record your current expenditures.

Some expenses, such as clothes, can be cut drastically when you're no longer dressing for success. Others like food and shelter will be more or less the same.

Delaying Retirement

As a general rule, you can assume that the longer you wait to draw on your various retirement income sources, the more money you will have. In other words, your retirement accounts will continue to earn interest and your annuities will yield higher returns. Boomers born in 1943 or later can boost their Social Security income by 8 percent for each year that they delay retirement up to the age of 70. On the other hand, they must take a penalty if they collect before they reach full retirement age. Research indicates that few boomers have saved adequately for retirement, so this is one very powerful incentive for remaining gainfully employed.

Remember that you will need to plan for a long and active life. It's hard for young people to imagine being old and so, when you were in your 20s, you may have imagined that you'd be dead and gone before you reached your 60th birthday. Even though this seems ludicrous now, you still may not be looking far enough ahead. Although you may have arrived at the ripe old age of 60 and anticipate going strong for years to come, you may not have considered just how many years. There is a reasonable chance that you will reach the age of 95. Although this is well above the average life expectancy, there are still many of you reading this book who will still be chugging along.

That means that if you are now 60, your resources must be spread over 35 years. If you are similar to many boomers, you did not get serious about a savings program until fairly recently, so it is unlikely that you have accumulated 35 years' worth of assets. If, however, you decide to retire at age 70, you could maximize your Social Security benefits and your retirement savings would be spread over just 25 years. In addition, you'd have an extra 10 years to build up more resources. You might even consider postponing retirement until age 75 if you're in good shape and really enjoy your job.

How Much Risk Can You Afford?

Apart from remaining in your present job, most of the options open to you involve some risk. In general, the more financially secure you are, the more risk you can take on. How important is money to you? Would you be comfortable living more simply? How economical can you be without starting to feel sorry for yourself? If you think that you could manage on a lot less money, now is the time to find out if you are right. Begin immediately to cut expenses and keep track of your savings. Of course, most people can postpone some expenditures, but could you continue living on such a limited income for the next 20 or 30 years? If you leave your job to take another, how will this affect both your present income and your future financial security? If your combined sources of income including Social Security, pensions, and retirement accounts will yield less than two-thirds of your current income, some major changes in your lifestyle will probably be needed.

How Much Money Can You Count On?

The next step is to take an honest look at your present financial situation and your anticipated retirement income. Begin by considering what your income would be if you retired tomorrow. The following are some basic sources of income:

Social Security. Each year about three months before your birthday, the Social Security Administration sends you a report that lists your annual contributions and estimates the benefits to which you will be entitled when you reach different ages. This will give you a general idea of what to expect from this income source, but you may need more precise information.

The earliest possible retirement age is 62, but collecting benefits before you reach full retirement age will permanently reduce them. What is your current age? How long will it be until you become eligible for full benefits, and how much money would you be losing if you begin collecting benefits before then? If you were to quit your job tomorrow, would you be eligible to collect Social Security? The job of your dreams would very likely pay less than your present one. Could you manage on a lower salary and wait until you reach full retirement age to begin receiving benefits? Would it be worth the wait? It is a good idea to make an appointment at your local Social Security office to make sure you have your facts straight, because you may be working on unwarranted assumptions.

Pension benefits. In recent years, many employers have discontinued their traditional pension plans. Some have substituted retirement investment accounts and others have ceased to provide retirement benefits of any kind.

During the early years of your career, however, you were probably covered by several different pension plans. Let us say that you are 60 years old and have been employed for roughly 40 years. Perhaps you have worked for a dozen different employers, and at least some of them offered some kind of retirement plan. Even if you had a part-time job while you were going to college, you may have been included in your employer's pension program.

Many people neglect to withdraw their pension contributions when they move on to a new job. In the excitement of changing jobs, moving to a new home, and experiencing other disruptions, you may have forgotten all about your pension benefits. However, if your employment lasted for a specified period of time, your pension contributions may have become vested. This means that you became entitled to receive a pension when you reached retirement age. You are probably entitled to not only your own contributions but also those of your employer, plus the interest these funds have earned over the years.

Your changes of address were probably not reported to the pension fund's administrators, and they quickly lost track of you. It is well worth the effort to contact each of your previous employers to find out how pensions are administered and whether funds are being held in your name. The Internet will allow you to track down those employers and obtain their current addresses and telephone numbers. You may need to play detective, investigating mergers, buy-outs, and name changes, but it is usually possible to identify the appropriate office to answer your questions.

Pension Benefit Guaranty Corporation. If your pension plan is a defined benefit plan (a traditional pension plan that promises to pay a specific monthly amount to participants) from a privately owned company, you can obtain help from the Pension Benefit Guaranty Corporation (PBGC; *www.pbgc.gov*). This agency keeps track of people who are eligible for pension benefits and now guarantees the benefits of 44 million people participating in more than 31,000 pension plans. PBGC's Website's "Pension Search Directory" lists people who are entitled to pensions.

Your Investments

What other sources of income can you count on when you retire? Begin making a list of all your retirement accounts and how much each is currently worth. Then add other stocks, bonds, and mutual funds that you own. What about your other assets? List all your bank accounts, the contents of your safe deposit box, and any real estate investments you may have.

Misplaced accounts. As with pensions, it is sometimes possible to misplace retirement accounts. Because these investments are a recent development, you probably needn't go all the way back to your college days, but you should still think about what benefits your various employers offered. Some, for example, might have included stock shares as part of their benefit packages. Stock options have probably expired, but is it possible that you've squirreled away some old stock certificates? Even if you've lost them, it's still possible to track them down through the company that issued them or its parent company.

Unclaimed property. Unclaimed property is another source of money you might want to look into. In general, the dream of recovering thousands of dollars of your unclaimed property is just that: a dream. Nevertheless, here are some other sources of money that might be waiting for you:

- An old savings account.
- A safe-deposit box.
- A legacy from a distant relative.
- Forgotten stock certificates.
- Property deeds.
- A final paycheck that never reached you.
- Public utility deposits you never claimed.
- Apartment security deposits.
- Life insurance proceeds.

It's probably not worth putting a lot of effort into this quest, but you would still be wise to spend a little time going over your past moves and job changes, especially any that were sudden and hurried.

When a bank, public utility, or pension fund is unable to locate you, it usually must hold unclaimed property for five years, and then turn it over to the state. States normally must safeguard that property "unto perpetuality." If the state auctions off the objects, such as the contents of a safe deposit box, it must hold the proceeds of the sale for the box holder. Every state has an unclaimed property office and you can check with them to see if any property is being held in your name (all the names you have ever used, as well as any variations and misspellings that may have prevented you from being notified). To locate the office in your state, type "unclaimed property" and the name of your state into any search engine. These state databases are usually free, and, if you find your name, it's easy to complete the online claim form. Be sure to choose a Website that ends in ".gov" or ".us," because you are looking for an official state agency. Many legitimate and not-so-legitimate e-businesses will offer to find your undiscovered treasures, but it's easier and cheaper to conduct your own search.

As mentioned, risk is a big concern as you get older. If an investment tanks, you no longer have time to wait until it once again becomes profitable. Many experts recommend that you begin reducing volatile investments and increase more stable (but possibly less profitable) ones. This usually means selling off stocks and replacing them with bond funds, balanced funds, or certificates of deposit (CDs). Ask your banker or financial advisor about ways to stabilize your assets.

Adding It Up

By this point, you should have a complete list of the income that will be available to you when you decide to retire. It probably seems like a lot of money. Remember, however, that it must last you throughout the rest of your life. There's nothing worse than being old and poor. As you get older, you can anticipate many new expenses. Your medical costs will rise, and you will need a lot of help. That means you will be paying people to perform services, such as house cleaning and lawn mowing, that you can no longer do yourself.

So how much of your nest egg can you spend each year without exhausting it? Let's imagine that in addition to Social Security, you've accumulated just $150,000 in assets. Retirement planners advise spending no more than 4 percent of your assets in the year you retire and increasing that amount only slightly in later years. That means that you will be living on Social Security plus $6,000. The average Social Security check is about $950 a month, or $11,400 a year. Face it! This is not enough to live on. If your assets add up to $300,000, then you can safely draw $12,000 out of your nest egg. You're still going to need more money to live comfortably. Where will you find more money?

Proceeds from the sale of a home. If you are similar to many people, you bought a house or condominium as soon as you were able to scrape together the required down payment. Through the years, you sent off your monthly mortgage payment and maybe used your home equity to purchase other houses that met your changing needs. National Realtor Coldwell Banker conducts an annual survey of home prices in their markets. In 2005, the average price of a single family home had risen to $401,767, up 13.3 percent from the previous year. If you own a home and have been making payments all these years, your equity may be close to this amount. One of the biggest decisions that confronts you is whether you want to keep this money tied up in a house or whether you want to use it for other purposes.

Making your home equity work for you. As you are making your plans, it's a good idea to think of money as power in the sense that it can give you power over your own life. The equity in your home can be used in many ways, some of which can actually alter your future. Many people either keep their homes until they are no longer able to live independently or plunk all that equity into another home. Bob and Sarah, however, had a different idea. Their children were grown and they no longer needed all that space just for themselves. Although they were both healthy and active, they knew that their tri-level house would not meet their future needs. Together they made a list of the kind of space they would need to pursue their hobbies and lead active lives during the years ahead. A smaller house would need less maintenance, and one that was all on one level would allow them to remain independent. Apartment living is a good option for many boomers because it frees them from many chores that burden homeowners, such as snow removal. However, Bob and Sarah decided to purchase a small single-family home instead. This time, however, they held back most of the proceeds from the sale of their home. Their down payment on the new house will be just large enough to keep their monthly mortgage payments affordable. The rest of the proceeds from the sale will go into an annuity or other low-risk investment that pays them a monthly living allowance. The extra funds will allow them to delay collecting Social Security until they reach full retirement age, as well as maximize pension and investment income. It will also give them the freedom to explore interesting job possibilities that pay less than their present jobs.

Maximizing your equity by relocating. Let's look at another example of a couple who sold their home. We'll call them Mr. and Mrs. Average. They're presently living in a suburb of Philadelphia where the average home price is $574,567. Because prices have been rising steadily and they have owned the house for 20 years, they owe only about $50,000 on their mortgage. Therefore, if they sold their house, they would have a net gain of about $525,000. What makes their situation even better is that they needn't pay tax on most of this money. A married couple can exclude up to $500,000 in profit from the sale of their main residence as long as they have owned it and lived in it for at least two years.

Rarely in our lives do we have this much money virtually at our fingertips. Of course, Mr. and Mrs. Average have to find someplace else to live. If they find it convenient to downsize their requirements, they might be able to buy another house in their area that meets their needs for $300,000. In that case, Mr. and Mrs. Average could make a down payment of $50,000 and continue to make roughly the same monthly payment. Now, however, they have $475,000 to put into an annuity or low risk investment, assuring them an income for the rest of their lives.

Mr. and Mrs. Average can actually do better than this if they are interested in relocating. Remember that they are selling their home in the Philadelphia area for $574,567. If they enjoy sunshine and ocean beaches, they might like to move to Wilmington, North Carolina, where the average price of a single family home is $286,650. If they would prefer the mountains, they might move instead to Billings, Montana, where the average price of a house is $142,500. Of course, Mr. and Mrs. Average no longer need as much space as they did when their children were younger, so they might find just what they want in Billings for less than the average

price. If they would like a bit of luxury, they might choose
a somewhat more lavish home that costs somewhat more.
Either way, after making the down payment, they will have
more than $500,000, enough to provide a permanent in-
come that will cover most of their needs. In fact, their lower
monthly mortgage payment and the lower cost of living in
Billings or Wilmington could mean that their money problems are over and they can pursue their interests without
ever having to worry about money again.

Developing a Plan

The goal of this chapter has been to give you a set of
building blocks to put together your own personal plan for a
rewarding lifestyle. Hopefully, you've clarified just what it
is you want to do with your life and how much money you'll
need to do it. Don't worry if you are still undecided about
some things. You've narrowed your choices and you've set
aside those rose-colored glasses that were making it hard to
estimate your financial resources. If you're similar to many
boomers, you've discovered that you can't expect to live comfortably for the foreseeable future unless you remain employed and postpone retirement. You've also come to the
realization that a job doesn't have to mean long hours of
boredom. It can become the focus of a happier, more meaningful lifestyle. Armed with all this self-knowledge, you're
ready to begin exploring both the opportunities and the challenges that await you out there in the job market.

2 Getting From Here to There: What's Holding You Back?

If you've done the soul-searching suggested in the last chapter, you've probably made a tentative decision. If that decision involves finding a new job that provides more satisfaction, friends, and other personal rewards, then it's time to get ready. You won't have an easy time of it, but you may have made one of the best decisions of your life.

This is not the time, however, to print a dozen copies of your resume and plunge into job-hunting. One of two things would probably happen. Most likely, your resumes would be greeted with an equal number of "thanks, but no thanks" responses (we'll talk about the reasons in a moment). If, for some reason the heavens looked favorably on you and you found a job, it would probably be little better than your old one.

Time to Get Ready

Instead of jumping into the fray immediately, take some time to prepare yourself. This does not mean quitting your present job. As you probably know from past experience, having to admit that you're unemployed can be the kiss of death when you're applying for another job. Consider carefully whether you can endure your present job for another six months or so. If you can, your transition will be a lot easier. If, however, you decide you can't, then there is no point in endangering your physical and mental well-being. You'll just have to accept the fact that your job hunt will be that much more difficult. It will not, however, be impossible, and your sunnier state of mind will counteract some of the negatives.

Seeing Your Workplace as a Laboratory

Let's say that you have decided to remain in your present job for the time being. This will give you a good opportunity to treat it as a kind of laboratory. If you've worked in the same kind of environment for many years, you will want to be sure you don't take it with you when you leave. After all those years, it may have become part of you. Have you internalized the competition and distrust that you're trying to get away from? At least part of what you experience on the job comes from inside you. To change your environment, you have to change yourself.

Getting to Know Yourself

So how do you know if a negative work environment has become part of you? Probably the best way to answer the question is to take a good look at the things you do outside of work. What about your leisure activities? Do you approach a club meeting or a weekend softball game in the same competitive way you approach work? Do you find yourself regarding friends, neighbors, and even family as obstacles or people who should be doing things your way?

If you're afraid the answer to these questions may be *yes*, try standing back and examining the way you relate with people on the job. When you feel your blood start to boil, back off! Take yourself out of the conflict. Force your blood pressure down and tell yourself it doesn't matter. You're a short-timer now, and you're here to prepare yourself for a more satisfying life. Each time you feel anxiety, fear, hostility, anger, or other strong negative emotions, take a good look at them. Most of us experience all these emotions in some work situations. They are partly generated by external factors such as an abusive boss or conflicting demands. However, they are also generated by our own, slightly neurotic selves. Many years in a "pressure cooker" environment can change your goals and values. Over time, a highly competitive focus on money and power can even change your relationships with people.

Don't Take the Pressure Cooker With You

When you resign or retire from your present job, it is essential to leave these neurotic attitudes behind, but that's a lot easier said than done. The only way to do it is to identify each of your negative behaviors and deal with them one by one. Use this time while you're planning the future to come to terms with yourself. Each time anger or jealousy surges up to the surface, try to understand what caused it. Then replace the anger with more mature, more positive thoughts. Look on your coworkers as human beings, not as competitors. Some boomers have found that once they changed their own attitudes, their jobs changed as well. If no one and no situation can make you feel stressed or angry, you may find you no longer need to make a job change.

Do You Enjoy Your Job?

Because you are using your workplace as a laboratory, start making lists of what you like and what you dislike about your job. At the end of a day, mentally review the hours you spent at work. When did you feel really involved in what you were doing? Which tasks gave you the most satisfaction, and which ones were downright unpleasant? Do many of the things you did during the day take advantage of your special talents? Do you have a real aptitude for the work? Would you say that, because of your unique talents, you can be more successful at these tasks than most people? If the answer to these questions is *yes*, then you're probably pursuing a career that meets at least some of your needs and just requires some tweaking.

You've Been Changing

If, however, you're starting to feel that you're a square peg in a round hole, then a change of scene will not solve your problems. Over the years, you have changed. You don't stop growing when you become an adult. Over the years, you have continued to change, and you've developed different aspects or parts of yourself that maybe you didn't even know about when you were a young job-seeker. In fact, when you were 18 or 19 choosing a college major, you probably knew very little about yourself. You were easily influenced by other people, as well as by books, television, and movies. Maybe you chose a career track because you especially admired a teacher, television personality, or other role model. Then again, you might have been told by your parents that you had all the makings of a doctor, clergyman, or whatever profession they wanted to see you take up. On the negative side, you may have been told by a teacher that you had no aptitude for a particular career. Whoever made this pronouncement merely meant that you did not resemble his or her image. This person, who may have changed the course of your life, probably knew little about you and your unique talents.

Because we know so little about ourselves when we're young, we tend to believe what we are told and proceed accordingly. As you look back on your work life, can you see a turning point, a point at which you made a choice that, in a sense, stopped you in your tracks? A choice that kept you from exploring other, possibly more satisfying, careers?

Exploring New Territory

Are you one of the many boomers who are dissatisfied with their jobs but are not quite sure what you would like to be doing? After an active career, retirement does not sound appealing, but maybe you have only vague notions of what kind of work you would really like to do. If you look carefully, you'll find many clues in your own life experiences. Examine your past successes, both in your personal life and in your work life; patterns should start to emerge. You were happier and more productive in one job than another. You need an organized environment to be effective—or maybe you're just the opposite and enjoy a looser, less-structured job with fewer rules and more room to express your individuality. Do you like to work alone, or are you at your best when you're part of a team?

Although examining your past can be a very productive exercise, you are also limited by your experience. What else is out there? If you had chosen a different path, would you have been happier? Because you can't turn back the clock, there's no way to know for sure. However, there are ways to peek into other people's experiences. You might ask, for example, which careers are the best fit for people like you.

Interest Inventories and Other Career Tests

Because no list of jobs has ever been created with your name on it, you will have to settle for somewhat less personal information. There is, however, a category of psychological tests called "interest inventories" that comes close to providing such a list. The best known is the "Strong Interest Inventory." To create the test, the publishers have identified thousands of people who report that they are happy and successful in their chosen occupation. They are then given a test that brings out their interests and attitudes, not their skills. Over the years, many, many people have taken the test and so there is now a profile of a typical man or woman in each occupational area. Your responses to the test questions are compared to the profile of a typical male forest ranger or a typical female tax attorney. The test pays almost no attention to whether you have the physical stamina for the outdoor job or the intelligence to pass the bar exam. A Catholic can score high on the scale for a rabbi even though he or she may know nothing about the Jewish religion. Despite this apparent deficiency, interest inventories turn out to be surprisingly good predictors of success in most occupations.

In addition to interest inventories, a wide variety of tests have been created to help people select careers. One of the great fringe benefits of enrolling in your local university or community college is access to their career counseling services. Many offer professional testing free of cost or for a very reasonable fee. You might ask about the tests available and the information you can glean from each.

There are also a number of tests available on the World Wide Web, and it is possible that one or more of them will alert you to a side of your personality you were not aware of. For example, the Career Key (*www.careerkey.org*) offers a well-designed career test for $7.95, and the Monster job board (*www.monster.com*) has a free but very short test based on the Myers-Briggs personality inventory. However, if you have the opportunity to obtain professional career counseling, you will probably be happier with the outcome. Just be careful, however, that you don't inadvertently encourage your counselor to tell you what you should do. You are looking for objective information, not a substitute for that teacher or family member who influenced your youthful career choice.

Reviving Your Dreams

Maybe over the years you have occasionally remembered a youthful dream and wondered if you should act on it. However, each time you considered living your dream, you backed off. You decided that you had advanced too far on your present career ladder to start all over again. Maybe right now, as you consider a job change, that dream remains stubbornly in the back of your mind. You're too old, you argue, to take up a new career. It would be easier to pick a low-stress job to keep you busy until you finally decide to retire. But a whole new career? It would take years and involve a huge amount of effort.

Maybe you're not entirely prepared to commit yourself to such a huge undertaking. There really are a few careers that are best begun when we're young and able to burn the midnight oil every night. More likely, however, the career you have in mind requires a reasonable amount of effort and commitment, but will not demand more than you have to give.

Lil's Story

I have a very good friend who decided on a career at the age of 60. In fact, she decided to change her whole life. Lil realized that remaining with an alcoholic husband was not helping either of them. With her children grown, she could either maunder over what might have been, or do something constructive to change her life. She chose to divorce her husband and go back to the university she had left at the end of her freshman year. The dream she had abandoned so many years earlier was to become an architect, and the path toward professional licensure is an especially difficult one. Resurrecting skills that had been dormant for 40 years was no easy task. Living on the wages of a work-study student wasn't easy either, but she realized that she could do it. Sure, she was stressed, but she was having fun, too. Sometimes she had to wrestle with her wayward short-term memory, but she also felt invigorated, as if she were fully alive for the first time in a long while.

Lil is 90 now. Of course, we all don't live to this ripe old age, but people who know her are convinced that Lil's career decision was as much responsible for her longevity as her healthy genes. Thirty years is a long time. It was time enough to graduate from college, earn a master's degree, and pass her licensure exams. It was time enough to apprentice with a local architecture firm, become a full-time architect, and, when she began to find the job too tiring, reduce her commitment to half-time.

Nowadays, Lil is no longer designing houses, but she's still involved with her firm. She says she just putters around. The youngish senior partner says she's taken on dozens of small tasks that keep the firm running smoothly. Lil has a variety of physical complaints, including an artificial hip that bothers her in cold weather. If she doesn't want to take a chance on icy sidewalks (she fell last winter, so she's still a little nervous), she submits her CAD files by e-mail. Computers, she says, are the bane of her existence, but she's learned what she needs to know to get the job done. The college student across the street helps her out when she has a real crisis or when she gets a strong urge to do violence to her PC. When Lil isn't working, she's driving city hall to distraction with her plans for neighborhood revitalization. Repeatedly, her city neighborhood has been threatened with demolition, and each time Lil has led her neighbors to victory.

Lil is unusual. She was probably an extraordinary person when she was 20. She just never had an opportunity to throw herself and her considerable talents into a project that really challenged her. The message her life sends out, however, is as valid for you as it was for her: Life is not over at the age of 60. We have no idea how many years we have left, but 30 years is a very long time to sit in a rocking chair, dreaming of what might have been.

What Makes You You?

But let's get back to you and the things you like to do. Do you enjoy working alone on a project, or do you prefer having other people involved? Does working as part of a team improve your work, or does it interfere with your concentration? Do you enjoy being with others and need frequent social interaction, or would you like to close your office door and focus on a task? Few of us are complete "loners," and neither are we social butterflies who can't stand to be alone. These are extremes, and most of us fall somewhere on a scale. Where you are on that scale has a lot to do with your comfort level. It would probably be a good idea to choose a job that allows you to have as much or as little contact with other people as you like.

Is a Part-Time Job Right for You?

Because you're using your present job to learn more about your needs and preferences, take a good look at the part-time staff. As you already know, they have little power or prestige. They may occupy a lowly place in the office status hierarchy, but they often have a more positive attitude than full-timers. They are not insiders and have no political standing. Therefore, they tend to remain more immune to office infighting. They have more time to spend in their private, personal worlds and so their jobs are not the central focus of their lives. They can usually put on their hats and coats and leave the office behind, taking with them plenty of energy to spend on leisure activities.

On the other hand, they probably don't receive the same benefits you do. They may not be entitled to sick leave, vacation time, health insurance, or the other perks that come with a full-time position. If you had a similar job, how would you manage? Most people find part-time work to be the best of both worlds if they can afford it. Can you? Are you eligible for Medicare or will you be eligible when COBRA runs out? Does your state provide a health insurance plan for people who are not covered by their employers' group plans? Have you looked into clubs and associations that make health insurance available to their members?

Many pension programs allow you to gradually increase the amount of money you receive each month so you can begin with a small monthly check that supplements your part-time wages. In fact, sometimes all you really need is the interest your account is earning. As you get older, you gradually receive a larger sum to compensate for your decreased earnings and the higher cost of living. Talk with a representative from your pension plan or a financial planner. You'll probably discover that you have more options than you realized.

Exploring Other Work Schedules and Benefit Options

When you were making career decisions those many years ago, your options were few. You worked the traditional 40-hour work week (which may actually have amounted to 60 or more hours if you took your work home at night) or you worked the shifts to which you were assigned. Either you had a full-time job or you were hoping for one. Today's options are more numerous and you should give careful consideration to any that interest you. Here are just some possibilities:

- ⊷ Flextime.
- ⊷ Compressed work week.
- ⊷ Job reassignment.
- ⊷ Job redesign.
- ⊷ Temporary/substitute jobs.
- ⊷ Job-sharing.
- ⊷ Phased retirement.
- ⊷ Telecommuting.

Employers are finally realizing that one size does not fit all, and so there are many more options available than when you were a young job-hunter. Investigate some of these different arrangements and decide if any are right for you.

Must You Be a Somebody?

Does the idea of sinking to a lower rung of the status ladder bother you? Does your ego rebel at the thought of being a "nobody" again? Nearly all of us have an older friend or relative who wants everyone to know that he or she used to be somebody important. My own personal story concerns Jim, but you could probably substitute half a dozen names of friends or acquaintances. Only the particulars would be different.

During his career, Jim held a number of important jobs in big companies. Unlike many, he was able to retire early and take advantage of a very generous severance package provided by his last employer. Instead of being delighted with this golden opportunity to live the life of his dreams, Jim's ego couldn't quite adjust to the change. All those years he labored in Corporate America, he was gradually absorbing a set of values that had no connection with real life. Everyone in his company had a precisely defined place in the pecking order. Within the company, that was all that mattered. You were seen as a valuable human being only if your position measured up. Over the 30 years of his work life in Corporate America, Jim gradually came to see his status at work as a kind of report card on his whole life.

When Jim retired, he brought those same values home with him. As he set about filling his time with interesting activities, he felt impelled to repeat again and again the details of his career and the important positions he had held. When he applied for a part-time job, he merely annoyed the interviewer by sending out signals that he was too good for the job.

The Story of a Nobody

My friend Walter, on the other hand, delighted in being a "nobody." Walter was very important in my life and remains my role model for growing old gracefully. Walter's career was a successful one and he eventually became superintendent of schools for a large district. Although it was a highly competitive environment, Walter always managed to have a good time. However, in those years retirement was automatic at the age of 65, and Walter found himself put out to pasture.

I don't honestly know what really happened then because Walter had so many funny stories about how he found his part-time job in the local college library. In one story he told frequently, the library director found him panhandling on the street and took pity on him. However he came upon it, the job was certainly no plum. It was a boring, half-time position gluing labels into books and doing other similarly mindless tasks. Walter, however, decided he was going to have fun. He was going to enjoy this job and he was going to be himself in a way that had never been possible when he supervised hundreds of employees.

Walter exulted in being "nobody." He did a reasonable amount of work but what he really excelled at was being with people. He enjoyed his coworkers and delighted in the students and faculty who came into the library. As time went on, it was gradually realized that Walter's many talents were being wasted. Because he was a born storyteller, he was asked to give tours to the Elderhostel and other groups that frequently visited the library. Walter continued to take pleasure in being a "nobody," however, and the new responsibilities never altered his enjoyment or his sense of the ridiculous. Working only part-time allowed him to remain at the job for many years, well into old age. As time went on, Walter became somewhat feeble and his short-term memory often failed him. However, his skills as a raconteur only improved and the laughs only got louder from the groups he so skillfully entertained.

Not everyone can be a Walter, and the choices he made may not be right for you. A part-time job isn't for everyone, but examine the possibilities carefully before you discard the idea. If you decide you need the benefits or income or prestige of a full-time job, maybe you can still find more time to recharge your batteries, and more energy and enthusiasm for leisure activities. If you can retrain yourself to remain comfortably on the same rung of the ladder, you may be able leave your work behind in the evening and start having fun.

The Story of a "Hard-Charger"

Each of us began life as a unique individual and the years have shaped us into fully formed adults. The same "you" who has been working all these years will be the "you" who makes these life changes. You'll have plenty of opportunities to work on your bad habits, but don't expect that you will somehow turn into a different person. Maybe Mel's story will illustrate this point. Mel ran away from home and joined the Navy at the age of 16. He'd had a rough home life with an abusive father, and he learned to survive the hard way.

After harrowing wartime duty, Mel found himself back in civilian life without even a high school diploma. By sheer determination and willpower, he earned a GED and worked his way through college. The drive and aggressive personality that had gotten him through childhood kept him alive through the war and propelled him through college were exactly the qualities needed to be a success in the corporate world. Life had made him intensely competitive and though his bosses might be uncomfortable with his "take no prisoners" attitude, he always managed to get the job done.

Though he rose to the position of senior vice president in a large company, he was not so successful in private life. Both his wife and his children resented his authoritarian style. By the time his youngest entered college, he was on bad terms with the entire family, and years went by when he had little contact with his children. If you were to ask Mel about his family, he would tell you he was entirely to blame. Although he was a responsible parent and a good provider, he was never able to leave the hard-driving executive behind at the office.

Mel arrived at retirement age with few prospects for a happy future. An angry turf battle resulted in his being ushered out the door with a financial settlement that would make most of us green with envy. He had never given retirement a thought but, in less time than it takes to tell it, he decided he would move to Florida and devote his life to fishing. You can probably guess how long that lasted. Of course, he was not suited to such a life. In six months, he was back at work, this time in a brokerage house, where he put his considerable talents to work and quickly made another pile of money. Once again, his colleagues resented his power plays, and Mel decided to quit while he was still ahead.

Now Mel had more money than he needed but little satisfaction. There was, however, one ray of sunshine: It turned out that he was a pretty good grandfather. Although his children still kept their distance, they gradually agreed to send their offspring to see Grandpa a few times a year. Somehow, he could communicate with his grandchildren in a way that had never been possible with his own children.

Mel tried out dozen different hobbies, clubs, and volunteer jobs, none of which really satisfied him. His hard-driving personality isolated him from his neighbors and, though successful in business, he was rarely liked. However, Mel's affection for children grew steadily; this seemed to be the only aspect of his life that was working. The best part of his week was the time he spent volunteering at the local children's hospital. After several years as a volunteer, however, Mel learned that the hospital might close. A major funding source had dried up and costs were increasing.

One day at the grocery store, Mel picked up a jar of Newman's Own spaghetti sauce. You're probably familiar with this company begun by film star Paul Newman. Its products are known for quality, but it differs from other companies in that all profits are donated to charity. Inspired by a sudden idea, Mel went home and called Newman's Own corporate offices. For a week, he drove the staff crazy getting more complete information. Then he took his idea to his amazed attorney and the rest, as the saying goes, is history. Seventy-five-year-old Mel started a successful e-commerce business with his teenage grandson as second in command. After each annual audit, all profits are turned over to the children's hospital. Mel is no different than he ever was, and it's fortunate his grandson has inherited his personality. Their battles are legendary, but both the business and their relationship are doing just fine. Although Mel's company isn't the only source of revenue that is keeping the hospital afloat, it's making a huge contribution to the health and happiness of many sick children.

In the end, Mel finally managed to find his way to a job and a lifestyle that was right for him. It would have been better, however, if he had taken a good, hard look at his strengths and weaknesses many years earlier. If he had understood himself better, he might not have wasted so much time making himself miserable. If the truth were known, Mel had become tired of corporate life long before he was nudged out the door, but he had never known anything different. He had chosen his road and single-mindedly ignored all the byways that connected with it. His life had been spent struggling to climb to the next rung of the ladder.

Taking Stock

Do you feel self-confident when you're at work? Does it seem to you that you're doing a good job and other people know it? Are you "in the loop"? In other words, do you know what's going on, and do you play an important role in advancing your organization's goals?

Learning From Younger People

As we get older, we sometimes start to feel marginalized. It seems as if everyone else is headed in a different direction and no one has given us the map. Social and work groups have formed around us and we don't really feel a part of them. It may be time for you to make a conscious effort to get back into the mainstream: cement work relationships, reestablish friendships, and generally become more aware of what's going on around you.

If you've been feeling you're somehow out of step, it's time for you to find out what's really going on at work. To at least some extent, what's going on there is happening in thousands or even millions of businesses all over the country. If you've been working for the same employer for a number of years, you may not like some of the changes that have occurred. Members of Generation X tend to have a very different attitude toward their jobs than boomers, and it's natural to feel somewhat critical. These are your colleagues, however, and you needn't agree with them all the time to enjoy their company. Their skills, education, and interests are all different from those of older workers. Your workplace is your laboratory, so learn more about these younger people. Are there ways you can communicate with them more easily? Can you add a few of their expressions to your vocabulary or express more interest in their conversations?

Although they lack your experience, younger people have an instinctive understanding of today's job market that you need. You want to understand what they know and what skills they have that you don't. These are the skills employers are looking for nowadays. Face the fact that employers may look at you as an old fogy who hasn't kept up with the times. How are younger people different? Of course, you are who you are, and there's no point in trying to transform yourself into another person. However, younger people fresh out of college come equipped with skills you lack, among the most important of which are probably computer skills. You may feel as if you're surrounded by annoying know-it-alls who pepper every sentence with computer jargon. You may also feel you're being patronized by youngsters who never explain anything clearly, but simply punch a few computer keys when you ask a question.

These kinds of experiences can make anyone computer-phobic. However, computers can enhance both your work life and your personal life. They are not just for young people and, if you make the effort, you will probably become a reasonably accomplished computer user. Hand-eye coordination is one of the few areas in which young people really excel over their senior colleagues, and this is probably what's giving you trouble. Face the fact that you didn't learn to use computers in school and you will definitely be slower and have less dexterity than younger people. Asking questions is the best way to learn, but you may not want to display your ignorance by asking too many questions. Maybe it's time to begin taking some computer courses at your local community college.

Do You Look the Part?

While you're becoming more aware of your younger peers, take a closer look at their clothing and hairstyles. What do they see when they look at you? Maybe it's time for you to bite the bullet and consider making some changes in your appearance. You might, for example, take a good look at yourself in a full-length mirror. Do you look your age or maybe even older than your age? Even more important, do you look as if you don't really care how you look? We live in a culture that tends to judge people, at least to some extent, by looks. Of course a 60-year-old man or woman won't resemble a movie star, but careless grooming, a pot belly, and out-of-style clothing can doom a job search.

Once you've gotten a clear picture of yourself on the job, it's a good idea to think back to other jobs as well. As you think about your career, do you see a little of Lil or Walter in the way you approached your work, or are you more similar to Mel? If you intend to continue working for the foreseeable future, being honest with yourself now is essential to your happiness. You're old enough and wise enough see yourself as you are, both your strengths and your weaknesses, but you've also had time to develop dozens of tricks to avoid facing them honestly. One of the peculiar things about us as human beings is that we're almost as likely to ignore our positive qualities as our negative ones. If the discoveries you've been making about yourself include roughly the same number of positive and negative aspects, you're probably being reasonably objective.

In the next chapter, we'll be focusing on the realities of today's job market. To cope with them effectively, you will need to know what you have going for you and what flaws can be easily corrected. Sure, it's hard to be that honest with yourself; however, the rewards so far outweigh the discomfort that you can't afford not to.

3   Understanding What You're Up Against

Now that you have a better idea what you want to get from a new job or new career, what can you expect when you reenter the job market? If you've been job-hunting recently, it won't come as a big surprise. However, if you've worked for the same employer for 10 or more years, you may have an unpleasant shock awaiting you. Many boomers and seniors report that that their applications are repeatedly overlooked. Applicants whose qualifications can't compare with their own are chosen for jobs. Would they have a case if they charged age discrimination? Probably not, unless the employer has clearly hired someone who does not meet published qualifications. More likely, the employer has seemingly good reasons for choosing an applicant and has been careful to word the job description to provide a lot of latitude for deciding onthe right person for the job.

Knowing What They Want

What is it that employers are looking for that these older applicants don't appear to have? What is it that sometimes makes a greenhorn college graduate more attractive to an interviewer than someone with proven abilities? You might say, at this point, that the reason boomers don't get the job is discrimination, pure and simple, and you may be right. However, it's almost never "pure and simple," and righteous indignation will not get you very far. Maybe this is a good time to make it clear that this book is not really about defending your rights or pursuing legal remedies when you have been unfairly denied a job. If you have specific reasons for believing that you are the victim of discrimination, then you need to discuss your situation with an attorney.

Many people who have sued an employer or sought justice from the Equal Employment Opportunities Commission say they feel no sense of accomplishment or satisfaction even when they win their cases. By the time they've invested one to two years of their lives, paid their legal fees, and dealt with stress-related health problems, they have little to show for their effort. Yes, it's true that employers may be more careful next time. Wary of age discrimination suits, they will more effectively conceal their real reasons for choosing particular applicants. Remember, however, that this is a guerilla guide. It is focused on success. Your goal is to get what you really want, and a year of anger and unemployment is not what you have in mind.

For the time being, you're going to forget about your rights. You're going to begin with the assumption that an employer will usually hire the applicant of his or her choice and you're going to become that applicant. Your experience and expertise will of course be important, but you're also going to become savvier. Guerilla job-hunters decide what they want and make an honest, objective assessment of what it will take to get it. If this means a little psychology, a little subterfuge, and even a little acting ability, so be it. If all your efforts fail, then it may be time to begin thinking about your rights.

Looking on the Bright Side

There is, however, a sunnier side to the picture. As a baby boomer, you are part of a huge population group. The first boomers born in 1945 are nearing retirement age. Soon employers will discover that boomers constitute such a substantial part of the workforce and it isn't so easy to replace them. The generation coming up behind the boomers is a smaller one and can't be expected to fill each and every vacancy. Eventually this will give you more bargaining power, but at present, the higher-paying, more desirable jobs are still attracting plenty of applicants. You may discover, however, that if you set your sights somewhat lower, there are a number of less competitive openings that are already being affected by the aging workforce. You may possess more bargaining chips at this level than you realize, and it may even be possible to negotiate more attractive benefits or a work schedule better suited to your lifestyle.

Stereotypes About Older Workers

Nevertheless, age discrimination is widespread in our society. Younger managers tend to look for other people like themselves. They imagine the way they would do a job and then seek applicants who match that mental picture. To be successful, you will want to fit that image whenever possible. In many respects, this really isn't so very difficult, because it is possible to make small adjustments in the image you project. However, you are who you are, and you'll never be 30 again. When superficial changes aren't enough, your task is to change the picture, emphasizing the positive qualities you will bring to the job and de-emphasizing the negative ones. Here are some of the stereotypes you are likely to encounter as you tweak this image.

The Americans With Disabilities Act

Younger people sometimes assume that anyone who has a disability is unhealthy. The law is clear that you can't be denied a job if your disability doesn't interfere with your job performance. Although legal action is usually a less-than-satisfactory solution, it is sometimes possible to gently remind employers of their legal responsibilities. The ADA, as the act is usually called, prohibits employers from discriminating against qualified applicants because of a disability. If you have a disability, you are entitled to certain accommodations on the job. A potential employer cannot assume that you will be unable to perform the job without giving careful consideration to the ways in which the work environment can be modified to meet your needs. Unfortunately, an employer is unlikely to tell you that he or she is making these assumptions, so you must decide whether to confront the problem head-on. This can be a difficult call to make. On the one hand, you will not want to call attention to your disability. Because you want to appear as similar to the employer and the other applicants as possible, you try to appear youthful and healthy. On the other hand, most employers have little experience dealing with disabilities and they may be laboring under unwarranted assumptions.

Application forms often include a question about whether you will require any special accommodations to perform the job effectively. Because you must answer this question honestly, the decision may be taken out of your hands. Many people with disabilities say that they prefer to be totally honest. They mention the disability and the accommodation they require, but they do so lightly. They do not invite sympathy or pity. Instead, they make it clear that they have already dealt with the issue and they are fully in control of their lives. Younger people who have never experienced ill health may find the topic upsetting. If it does not appear to be upsetting to the applicant, they are more likely to approach it in the same way.

In general, ADA noncompliance can be proven much more easily if you are already on the job and your employer lets you go, demotes you to a lower paying job, or refuses to promote you. When you're applying for a new job, the employer has a lot of discretion. However, when requirements are clearly listed in the job announcement and/or the job description, an employer usually may not hire an under-qualified applicant when a fully qualified applicant is available. If you can prove that this has occurred, you may have a good case. Unfortunately, "real life" situations are not usually this clear. Listed qualifications are usually divided into two categories: "required" and "desired." The list of required qualifications is kept fairly short, whereas the desired qualifications may be a lengthy laundry list. As long as applicants can reasonably claim to possess all the qualifications listed on the short "required" list, an employer can more or less pick and choose among the "desirables."

Older Workers Are Unhealthy

Of course, we tend to have more medical problems as we get older, but there is plenty of evidence that this does not usually affect on-the-job performance. In fact, older workers use no more sick leave than younger ones, and, in many cases they use less. Nevertheless, you may unconsciously be reinforcing this stereotype by your behavior on the job. For example, sharing information about your health with your colleagues is not usually a good idea. When someone asks you how you are, your usual response should be "fine" or, in recent parlance, "I'm good." Of course, you worry about your health, but these worries should generally be shared only with your family and close friends. Sometimes you get into the bad habit of talking about your health when you can't think of anything else to say. In fact, if you're perfectly honest, sometimes you just enjoy talking about yourself. Instead of letting the conversation focus on you, ask a question. Express more interest in what your colleagues have to say.

Looking fit and healthy. The other day, a friend was telling me about his high school reunion. He was amazed at how much his classmates had changed. An outsider would never guess that everyone was the same age. Some of them looked as if they were in their 40s; others might have been 70 or more. Sometimes ill health ages us prematurely, but more often there are little things that we do or don't do that make us look old. For example, women who wear a moderate amount of makeup usually look younger than those who plaster it on with a trowel or who wear no makeup at all. Men may develop a permanent slouch that adds years to their age.

Are you overweight? Many studies have proven that employers discriminate against applicants who are overweight. They assume a greater likelihood of health problems (true) and a lower energy level (frequently, but not always, true). As we get older, we tend to gain a pound or two every year. This is because our metabolisms slow down but our eating habits tend to remain unchanged. Extra weight can make us seem much older than we are. When we huff and puff after a short walk or a flight of stairs, we send out a message that we are no longer healthy and active. Overweight men and women often walk and sit differently from physically fit ones, so they are constantly sending out negative messages.

When boomers were young, the standards for calculating ideal weight were much different than they are today. A man or woman could weigh considerably more and still not be considered obese. Younger people have grown up with the new standards, and they view others as being overweight if they don't meet them. In fact, today's fashion dictates a very slim silhouette. Don't spend your time mentally accusing your colleagues of being anorexic. Find out what your weight should be, based on these newer standards that are the result of exhaustive medical research. Decide what you can do to bring your weight into line, and don't use your age as an excuse.

Developing healthy habits. Before you begin job-hunting in earnest, get a thorough medical checkup. Take control of conditions that could interfere, not only with your new job, but with your new life. Make time for vitamins and supplements that might help you feel more alert. Add regular exercise to your schedule and stop inventing excuses to avoid walking or taking the stairs.

Do you smoke? Of course, smoking is a major health risk, but I've also been told by younger people that they find it disgusting to see older people smoke. They describe them standing outside their office buildings puffing a fast cigarette while they shiver in the cold. These uncomfortable smokers seem pathetic and undignified. I don't quite know why younger smokers aren't equally disgusting, but, if you ask some of your younger friends, they are likely to say the same thing.

Older Workers Don't Have Any Energy

This is one of those stereotypes that are half true and half false. Your energy level usually does go down as you get older. However, most of us are not ready for the rocking chair. Your energy level is usually perfectly adequate for most jobs if you maintain a healthy lifestyle. You must decide, however, how you want to expend your energy. When you were young, you might say you had energy to burn. You could work during the day and party at night. You could hold two jobs or work evenings and weekends to climb the ladder of success more rapidly.

Now you must choose how you will spend the energy you have available. For example, working full time may not leave you with enough energy for the other things you want to do. Take a moment to consider how you would like to spend a perfect day. Some people want nothing more than a relaxing evening at home after a day at work. Others want to participate in clubs, sports, or hobbies. For them, a part-time job might be a better choice. Think of energy as a pile of dollar bills. How can you divide them up to produce the most satisfying lifestyle?

The importance of exercise. When boomers were young, the importance of exercise was not fully understood. The latest research indicates that regular exercise adds about three years to your life. Contrary to what you would expect, exercise also increases your energy level. This is counter-intuitive; it seems as if we would be spending those energy dollar bills when we exercise, not getting them back, but it turns out that this is the case. People who establish a regular exercise routine and perform it three or more times a week find that they have more energy for both work and play. The key word here is *regular.* Create a routine that meets with your doctor's approval and that you can really stick to. Don't begin with an exhausting routine and then give up after a few days. Start off with short, easy sessions and increase only as your strength and stamina increase.

Midday slump. Boomers are not the only people who experience a slump in the early afternoon. However, as you get older, you become more aware of this downtime when you feel dull and sleepy. If you allow yourself to lose your momentum and slow down to a crawl during these hours, then you will definitely seem to be an old geezer to your younger colleagues. Your productivity will also go down because you won't be able to get all your work done. You don't live in a country where you can take a midday siesta, so you must find ways to remain alert throughout the day.

I've spoken to many successful boomers about this problem, and each has a slightly different solution. Many of their recommendations have something to do with lunch. They find that it is important to eat a light lunch to stabilize their body's glucose level. A big lunch often has the effect of making them feel "wiped out" and unable to get anything done for the rest of the afternoon. If they don't eat something, however, their "fuel" level drops, as do their eyelids. Some recommend a caffeinated drink (a cup of tea, for example) when they begin to feel their concentration waning. The main thing is that you get to know yourself. Try different strategies, such as taking a walk, eating a low-cal snack, or doing a few exercises at your desk.

Older People Are Know-It-Alls

Think back to your early years in the workplace. Do you remember an older employee who never wanted to change, never wanted to do anything differently? He or she had always done the job the same way. If it was good enough then, it's good enough now! Change is an essential part of life, but change is often painful. There is no question that as we get older, time passes more quickly, and the world sometimes seems to be changing so fast we feel as if we're on a spinning merry-go-round. Try to analyze your own response when someone at work suggests a new way of doing things. You may feel an automatic urge to oppose the change, especially if you were responsible for the present policy or procedure.

How it used to be. Boomers who have worked for the same employer for a number of years are also inclined to talk about the way things used to be. When managers or staff get together around a conference table to discuss a new idea, does your part in the discussion usually consist of a history of the way things were done in the past? Of course, it is certainly important to learn from past mistakes, but the environment is different than it was 10 or 20 years ago. New strategies are needed to deal with the world of today. If you can look back and hear your own voice whining, "We tried that and it didn't work" again and again, it's unlikely that you are "winning friends or influencing colleagues." This is a good reason to move on to a different job where you no longer have all that baggage to drag around. However, if your bad habits go deep, then, even when you have a new job and a new employer, you will still be tempted to trot out old stories.

Is it so important to you to be right that you keep insisting on your point when it is clear that the group is moving in a different direction? Of course, you have knowledge and experience that these younger colleagues lack. However, the moment they begin comparing you to their mothers of fathers, your on-the-job enjoyment will decline. After all, they don't want to take their parents to work with them.

What You Have to Offer

All this talk of stereotyping and discrimination may sound so depressing that you wonder what you really have to offer. Don't sell yourself short or let these misconceptions get you down. You have experience, both work experience and personal experience, which adds up to a real goldmine. Of course, much of your experience is with processes and procedures. However, the human side of any organization is even more important, and human nature doesn't really change. You've worked with hundreds of different people and you've learned a great deal about human nature. You have participated in untold numbers of meetings and you know how groups can get sidetracked. You have also seen groups work together to produce innovative solutions. Your intuition, based on your years of experience, is useful if you have a role in hiring new employees. You have a clearer picture of who's likely to do a job well and who will talk more and do less. You can even spot destructive patterns of behavior and keep your distance from interpersonal conflict. The word *wisdom* is a little high-fallutin' for this kind of book, but age does bring at least a little wisdom with it. You've seen more of life and recognize the signs of success and failure. Although history doesn't really repeat itself, your experience can provide an occasional peek into the future.

Use Your Noggin

Don't forget that you know more now than you did when you were 25. In other words, you've acquired a wealth of information about a zillion different subjects. Sure, you forget names and can never find your keys. This is your short-term memory making you miserable, but your long-term memory—in other words, most of that knowledge that you've acquired over the past 50 or so years—is there for your use, even when you can't pull up specific details.

To be successful, you'll need to get that long-term memory working overtime while at the same time keeping that wayward short-term memory under wraps. There are many books and articles that provide suggestions for dealing with short-term memory failures, but few mention long-term memory. When you tell those stories about the way things used to be, you're calling on your long-term memory in a way that does you little good. However, if you look closely, you'll discover that each of those stories contains an important lesson. When you're using the story to put down the innovative ideas of your colleagues, you're wasting one of your most useful tools. There's a lot more to each story than you're remembering. It is actually possible to mentally go back in time and watch different scenes unfolding. Why does one idea succeed when another fails? Look at the people in the story. Why is one so skillful at predicting the future while another always gets it wrong? Look at your own role in the story. Too often we tell stories just to show that we were right and the other guy was wrong, but there's a lot more to most stories than "I told you so!"

4 Deciding Where You'll Live and Work

Perhaps the most difficult choice that lies ahead is deciding how much of your life needs changing. As you think about a new job, are you imagining yourself living in the same house in the same community? If you have remained in your old job because it was the only one available, then maybe your community doesn't offer the scope you need. If part of your dream is to move to a sunnier climate, to a more welcoming community, or to a place with better educational and cultural opportunities, then there's probably no better time than the present.

It's Not an Easy Choice

Deciding where to live, however, is a much more complicated task than it might at first seem. Many baby boomers look on this phase of their lives as a transition between their old jobs and retirement. They want to have the best of both worlds: a regular paycheck and time to enjoy their favorite leisure pursuits. They are looking for a place that can offer both a job and an environment that meets their personal needs.

Recent surveys of baby boomers indicate that they are not only planning to work longer than earlier generations but are also planning to move to new communities that are more in tune with their lifestyles. Modern medicine has added many years to their life expectancies, and boomers want to make good use of them. Many are planning to relocate to communities where the cost of living is low, recreational opportunities are plentiful, and the environment feels as if it's custom-tailored to their unique needs.

So how will you decide whether to stay where you are or move to a new community? It's possible that you already know the answer to this question. If you want to remain near your family, you like your present home, the cost of living is moderate in your area, and the job market is good, you will very likely want to remain in your home community. If, however, your family is scattered and you live in a place you have never really liked, a new environment may be the best choice for you.

Consider the Cost of Living

Boomers are looking for places they can afford. If you are planning a job change to satisfy your changing interests and outlook, then it's best to plan for a lower salary. The cost of living in different parts of the country can vary so sharply that you might be forced to live in something approaching poverty in one area while you could be very comfortable in another. If you own a home in a coastal city such as New York or San Francisco, selling it and moving to a less costly area could provide not only funds for a new home, but also a significant increase in your disposable income. This might, however, mean leaving children and grandchildren behind. Alternately, if you are still maintaining a large house for one or two people, you could reduce both your worries and your expenses by moving to a smaller house. This might free up funds for a variety of enjoyable leisure pursuits. Now is the time to consider how important your present home is to your sense of happiness and well-being.

Consider Your Family and Friends

Do you play a large role in the lives of your children and grandchildren? Are daily family phone calls and weekly get-togethers an important part of your life? Has most of your family remained close by, or have they moved to distant parts of the country? Although there are still small towns where children graduate from high school or college, then settle down in their home communities, we have become a much more transient society. Nationally advertised job openings, the World Wide Web, and a tight job market are leading more young people to move away from their hometowns. You might choose either to follow them or set off on your own adventure.

Consider Your Options

Just as you used pen and paper to list the good and bad points of different lifestyle choices, take a few minutes now to consider the positives and negatives of moving to a new location. Remember, however, that you have many choices, each of which brings with it different attractions and different problems. Before you begin, let's list some of the choices available to you:

- Remaining not only in your hometown but also in your present home.
- Moving to a new home, possibly to a different neighborhood.
- Remaining within easy driving distance of your present hometown.
- Settling in another part of the country.
- Moving to another country such as Mexico or participating in a program such as the Peace Corps that might send you anywhere in the world.

Consider the Job Market

Now let's consider why you might choose any of these alternatives. How is the job market in your hometown? Is the unemployment rate above or below the national average? What kinds of jobs are available? Are jobs that interest you available? Are there a reasonably large number of local employers, or are you living in what might be called a "one-company town"? Because you're looking for a more satisfying life, you will need to be able to say *no* to jobs that will not help you achieve your goal.

Remember, too, that you are likely to have a more difficult time finding a job than younger applicants, so you probably can't count on just one or two possibilities. Get into the
habit of checking job openings in your local newspaper as
well as newsletters and Websites that cover your field. Keep
track of the number of interesting job openings for which
you are qualified. Do they come up fairly often? Even though
you're not ready to make a decision, it might be useful to
take some tentative steps now, putting out feelers and asking around about possible openings.

Weigh the Pros and Cons

Like most of us, you can probably find a lot of positive
things to say about your hometown as well as some negative
ones. How can you weigh the two sides? While you have
your pencil and paper close by, you might answer the following questions.

**•◦ Do you really like the area where you are
     presently living?**

Does it offer the kind of recreational activities you enjoy? Is it scarred by urban blight? Is there a real sense of
community?

•◦ Have you dreamed of moving?

Do you sometimes imagine a different lifestyle in another part of the country? Are you a frustrated outdoor person who's always lived in the city or an Easterner who dreams
of life on a cattle ranch in the Wild West? Some of these
early dreams were unrealistic and unlikely to provide the
happiness you seek. Others, however, are not such impossible dreams and can become practical realities with just a
bit of tweaking. Remember that your physical abilities are
different from what they once were, and you can expect
physical limitations to increase in years to come. Thus, a
lifestyle that involves a lot of hard, manual labor is probably
not the right one for you.

✱ Do you like the climate?

As you get older, Northern winters no longer mean snowmen and winter sports. They may come to mean agonizing snow-removal chores and painful falls on the ice. You needn't move to Florida to find a more congenial climate. Just gaining a month or two of milder weather when you can golf or take long walks may be well worth the effort. Cold weather should not be your only climate consideration, however. Many people move to the Pacific Northwest because of its attractive lifestyle and mild climate. Once they arrive, they discover that the sun may not shine for weeks or even months on end. For some people, sunlight is essential to their sense of well-being and its absence can bring on depression. Have you ever lived in this type of climate? If not, why not consider a vacation before you make any firm commitments?

✱ Has your neighborhood changed?

Has it improved or gone downhill in ways that concern you? Is it as safe as it used to be? Of course, the world in general has become less safe, but has your neighborhood become even more crime-ridden?

✱ Why did you choose your present location?

Jobs are often available in unappealing places. Sometimes when you can't find work in more pleasant spots, you tell yourself that it will just be a year or two. You'll stay only as long as it takes to pay off your bills or just until another job comes along. In time, you get used to the factory town or ugly suburb and never get around to leaving. Maybe you discovered that the place had unsuspected charms but if you still talk about leaving, there will never be a better time than now.

✱ Do you have a long commute?

If you are spending two or three hours a day driving to and from work, it's probably time for a change. These are precious hours that could be spent doing a variety of things that would enhance the quality of your life. It takes longer to recharge your batteries after age 60, and that leaves fewer hours to do the things you really enjoy. Spending hours locked in heavy traffic is not something most of us enjoy. It is neither quality time nor downtime when you can rest and restore your energy. You are not even being paid to commute, so you have to ask yourself, "What's the point?"

➖ Does your hometown have good public transportation?

Buses and trains have disappeared in many places. However, if you build a lifestyle around your ability to drive your own vehicle, you may be setting yourself up for failure. As a result of the large number of seniors involved in accidents, there has been a move in recent years to make it more difficult for seniors to renew their driver's licenses. Even if you are able to keep your license, you may find that your vision and reflexes are not what they used to be. It's best to be in a position to stop driving when you feel the time is right and still enjoy a satisfying lifestyle.

➖ How does the cost of living compare?

A friend who moved to a large city to be near her daughter was telling me how poor she feels. It seems to her she has not only moved to a new home but moved out of the middle class. Other people find themselves living much more comfortably in a new town, even though their actual income is unchanged. Because you are probably anticipating a salary cut, this is an important consideration. It may be possible to sell your home and buy a less expensive one in another area. That will give you extra money for investments and emergencies.

➖ Does living in a resort community appeal to you?

Have you always wanted to live at the beach where you can swim or sail whenever you like? Do you love the mountains and the quaint mountain towns of Vermont or Colorado? Resort areas have both their good and bad sides. For example, mountain resorts may be abandoned in the winter when snow and ice cause treacherous roads to become all but impassable. Nothing can be more depressing than a beach resort on a dreary winter day. Both, however, may offer more recreational activities. Remember that employment opportunities will be limited and, if you want to work, you may need to lower your sights to more mundane openings in the tourist industry.

◆ Are you still happy with your home?

When your children were young, you moved to the suburbs and mortgaged yourself to a single-family home. Do you still want to take care of that big backyard? It was great for the kids, but why do you need it now? Has climbing stairs become more of a chore, and is the house a whole lot bigger than it needs to be for just you and your spouse? Suburbia tends to be a great place for young families but not so desirable for middle-aged couples and singles. City high-rises may offer convenience and freedom from lawn maintenance. Country living may be more workable when you don't have to transport children to soccer practice and music lessons every day.

◆ What about your medical needs?

Do you or your spouse have a medical condition that requires easy access to an urban medical center? Sometimes small towns have surprisingly good medical facilities, but they can't provide the kind of specialization available in a more populated area. Even if you don't need medical care now, give some attention to the number of physicians and hospital beds near at hand. Boomers and seniors make more frequent use of medical facilities than younger people, and you don't want to drive 50 miles just to see a doctor.

Matching the Job to the Place

How come, you may ask, you're thinking about a new job and I'm writing about places to live? The reason is that you're making not only a job change but also a lifestyle change. Now that you have made the decision to trade your present job for a more rewarding life, you'll want to consider the other aspects of your life that make you feel discontent as well. If you are willing to move a few steps down the career ladder, the kinds of jobs you are looking for are probably available in many areas. This means that you can enjoy some of the pleasures of retirement while you are still working. If you plan to have more leisure time available, you may want to move to an area where you can make better use of it.

On the other hand, you may not be planning to ratchet down your work. Instead, you may want to launch a whole new career. In that case, location will be important for other reasons. You may want to relocate to be near a college or university. You may discover that job prospects in your new field are better in another part of the country. Even if there is no practical necessity to relocate, you may want to consider it as part of an overall plan to enhance your life.

Becoming a Snowbird

For a growing number of boomers, one location is no longer adequate. Although they continue to enjoy their home communities, they are no longer willing to remain trapped in their homes all winter, shoveling snow and worrying about treacherous ice. They want to enjoy the best of both worlds: their friends and family when the weather allows them to lead full and rewarding lives, and a balmier getaway destination where they can live every day to its fullest.

Although becoming a snowbird is, for many, a very attractive lifestyle, it is a complicated one. Imagine that your home is in Massachusetts and you dread each winter more than the last. Two years ago, you and the family spent a wonderful holiday vacation in the sunny Southwest and you've been dreaming of it ever since. Would it really be possible to enjoy the gorgeous fall color in your home state and then flee like a migrating bird to temperate Arizona? In spring, when Arizona is becoming uncomfortably warm, you could return home to be reunited with the family, friends, and other homey attachments you left behind.

Most experienced snowbirds will tell you that they love their lifestyle, but it's not as easy as it looks. They lead two almost entirely separate lives, and this means doubling both their planning and the inevitable complications. For example, they need two homes; what happens to each of them while they're gone? If they start a new job, what happens when it's time to leave? Must they be dishonest to employers or are there jobs that they can leave in the spring and return to next fall? What about their friends, their church, their medical care, and—perhaps even more difficult—their bank account? If you're wondering whether you would really like to try this enticing lifestyle, here are some questions to help you put your thoughts in order:

•❖ Can you afford to become a snowbird?

As a boomer, you probably need to continue earning at least part of your income. You are probably not a wealthy retiree who can maintain two sizeable residences without considerable strain on the pocketbook. As we will see, it is not only possible but also desirable to live simply and economically, but you will probably discover that the costs associated with becoming a snowbird are more than you might expect. For example, snowbirds must keep up rent or mortgage payments on two nests and pay two sets of utility bills. Their HMOs may not have branch clinics in their winter location, so they must pay additional medical expenses. Home insurance may be more expensive if the house if vacant more than 30 days.

•❖ Do you like to drive?

Snowbirds usually drive to each of their seasonal homes because they will need their car, truck, or SUV when they get there. Husbands and wives may each drive a vehicle if they will need both when they arrive. They are also burdened with personal possessions that they can't duplicate at each location, so any other form of transportation is usually expensive and inconvenient. This can mean two arduous, cross-country trips each year. As we get older, this kind of driving becomes less attractive for some of us. Other boomers enjoy the open road so much that they spend all or most of the year traveling in their RVs. Take a good, honest look at your driving habits and your health before committing yourself to the snowbird way of life. Retirement communities often have their own transportation, but you are probably anticipating both a more active and a less costly lifestyle.

•• Are you an extrovert or an introvert?

Extroverts who make friends quickly and easily tend to adjust well to snowbirding, as do introverts who don't need a lot of social interaction. Those of us who fall somewhere in the middle may find it hard to adjust to leaving our friends twice each year and having to reestablish relationships again and again. Some boomer snowbirds are amazingly good at this and feel they are blessed with twice as many friends and twice as many interests. It might be a good idea to try snowbirding for a season without making a permanent commitment. That way, you will be able to discover whether it meets your personal needs or if you are lonely and miss the people who mean the most to you.

•• What kind of jobs are you willing to consider?

Although there are a number of jobs that are suitable for snowbirds and it is even possible to work in both of your home communities, opportunities are more limited. Most available jobs are in the retail, tourism, and service sectors. Do these appeal to you? Most consultants can do their work from any location, but they usually do a lot of traveling. Some types of home businesses allow their owners to pack up their computers and take their businesses with them. In general, however, you will probably have to readjust your expectations to find employment. In later chapters, we will discuss the opportunities available to snowbirds, but, if you are wedded to a particular kind of job, you may find that you have to choose between a job and a balmy winter home.

•• How important is your family home?

Let's imagine that you own your own suburban, single-family home complete with trees, grass, sidewalks, and all the other accoutrements that are a part of the lifestyle. What will happen to your property when you flee to the Sunbelt? Suppose the hot water heater leaks or vagrants discover the house is empty? Roofs can also leak, and who will shovel those sidewalks? Remember that the public will be striding past your house just as usual and, if they should slip on the ice, you could be facing a very large lawsuit.

Many snowbirds hire a property management firm or arrange to have a snow-removal company take charge of the sidewalks. However, these solutions are rarely fully satisfactory. It's usually best to have friends or family check your house often. When snowbirds return, they leave behind a second home and a different set of potential problems. You might find that being chained to real estate spoils your enjoyment, so the simpler your accommodations, the better. Worrying also spoils your fun, so it's important to go, enjoy yourself, and don't obsess about what's happening elsewhere.

Consider, too, where you will live in your getaway community. Many snowbirds choose small apartments or trailer parks to save money. Because they are able to live a more active, outdoor lifestyle in the warmer climate, they are happy with less than sumptuous housing. Will this work for you? Will you really be spending most of your time working and playing under the sun? If the things you like to do are really indoor activities such as puttering in your workshop, collecting stamps, or playing on your computer, then such minimal accommodations might quickly get on your nerves.

➻ How warm must it be?

Resort communities often have a sameness that has both its good and its bad sides. For example, many Florida and Arizona communities attract large numbers of retirees. Would you enjoy their company or prefer more variety among your neighbors? There's a reason why the sun is nearly always shining in the Southwest: it doesn't rain. If you're an avid gardener, you may be unwilling to trade your moist, rich soil for an arid, sandy plot that can grow almost nothing but cactus.

If you're looking for a place that's more like home—just a little warmer—then you might look more closely at the states that lie more or less in the middle of the country. Think of these areas as the porridge in the story of "Goldilocks and the Three Bears": These areas are neither hot nor cold and neither North nor South. Colorado, for example, gets pretty cold, and snow is not uncommon. However, the sun shines so often and so brightly that ice melts quickly. In a drier climate with the sun beaming down on you, you are much less aware of the cold. The western part of North Carolina is another mountainous area that gets a real winter. However, it lasts for only a couple of months, compared to northern states where you can have a snowfall in June. If you're looking for a traditional small town, the Midwest, Midsouth, and Pacific Northwest have literally hundreds of charming places where winters are relatively brief.

Getting Inside Information

Whether you decide to stay close to home, explore another part of the country, or enjoy the best of both worlds, you will need information. If you decide to remain in your home community, it will be easier for you to learn about the kind of job openings you are looking for. You have friends who can tell you about the employers in the area. Their personal experiences can help you decide whether a job would provide the kind of work environment you are seeking or merely a return to the old grind. If you plan to leave your home community, however, you will need to learn about the job market from other sources.

Fortunately, it is a lot easier to learn about a distant community today than it was a few years ago. The big change that has occurred is the emergence of the World Wide Web. If you do not presently own a home computer, it is probably the best job-hunting tool you can get. Of course, you will probably need a computer to hone your skills for the job market, but a computer can also put you in touch with communities throughout the country and around the world.

Visiting the Chamber of Commerce

Let us say that you once drove through a town in New Mexico or Ohio or North Carolina. You found it attractive and it has remained in your memory. However, you really know nothing about it. In all probability, the area's chamber of commerce has a site on the World Wide Web. If you simply enter the name of the town and the word "chamber" into a search engine, you should be able to find it. Once you have surfed your way to the chamber of commerce, you will find an enormous amount of information.

Of course, the chamber has a somewhat biased point of view, but the basic information you need to start your exploration is right there. You should find data on climate, industry, employment, medical facilities, schools, and churches. There is almost no limit to what you can discover about a town if you read between the lines and let your imagination flesh out the dry statistics. How does this information compare and contrast with what you might find if you looked up your own hometown? In fact, it would be a good idea to look up your hometown chamber of commerce site, too, because you don't have your own statistics on the tip of your tongue. Is the unemployment rate higher or lower? Is there more or less snow? Does it seem that you would have more difficulty finding a doctor? Is the airport farther away? Is the cost of living higher?

The chamber of commerce site will also tell you about educational institutions in the area. Many boomers find that it makes a huge difference to their quality of life when there is a local college that sponsors plays and concerts, makes continuing education courses available to the community, and otherwise contributes to the quality of educational and cultural life. If you are changing careers, a local college can provide the kinds of courses that will prepare you for your new job and enhance your resume.

Another excellent source of information on the Web is the U.S. census. Both the population and business censuses will provide information you can use in reaching a decision. For example, the percentage of the population over the age of 65 can give you a useful insight into community life. Even seemingly irrelevant statistics such as infant mortality and heads of households can expand your mental picture of a place.

Your Public Library and Other Information Providers

In many cases, the best source of information is the site maintained by the local public library. Although some library Websites are not so fully developed, others provide links to dozens of information sources about their local area. I have also found that many local clubs and other organizations maintain Websites for the purpose of informing their present members and recruiting new members. From the articles you find on these pages, you'll get some idea of what community residents are like and how they spend their time.

One of the first pieces of advice that job counselors usually give their clients is to subscribe to the local newspaper. If you are interested in possibly moving to Middletown, subscribe to the *Middletown Gazette*. Of course, the immediate reason for the recommendation may be the "Help Wanted" ads, but there are many other reasons to subscribe to a local newspaper. All the issues of the day will be plastered across the front page, including insurrections against city hall and high school football scores. Real estate listings will give you an idea not only of housing costs but also of the economic condition of the area. When a new employer comes to town, it may make the front page, but the headlines are even larger when a business closes, leaving many local people out of work.

Your local public library has a number of books that provide information about the quality of life in different towns and cities. One of the best, *The Places Rated Almanac*, compares dozens of different "quality of life" indices (such as crime, public transportation, and medical services) and comes up with a composite rating for each city. By perusing such books, visiting a number of local Websites, and subscribing to the local newspaper, you are immersing yourself in a town to which you might relocate. It is almost as if you're visiting the place, but you can gather a lot more useful information than a tourist who visits only a few stores and restaurants.

Being on the Spot

Nevertheless, you might consider spending your next vacation checking out the towns that have caught your fancy. If you do your homework ahead of time and come prepared with information, you will be better able to interpret what you see. You might even consider making appointments with local employers. It's very possible that their telephone numbers and e-mail addresses will be available on the chamber of commerce's Website. In fact, the larger businesses may have their own Websites.

While you're visiting, try to imagine yourself as a resident. How would you spend your time? Would you have enough to do to occupy yourself? How would you describe the people you encounter? Of course, this is hardly a good sample of local residents, but it may give you some idea of economic, educational, and cultural characteristics. Spend some time with the local telephone directory. Is your religious affiliation represented by a church or synagogue? If so, you might attend a service and compare the people you meet with your home congregation.

Some communities are very difficult for outsiders to break into. For example, when we say a town is "unspoiled," we probably mean that new arrivals are rare and so the town is insulated from change. Local residents may think of you as different or odd. How much would this matter to you? If you are used to a very active social life in your hometown, you might begin feeling depressed if your new neighbors are unwelcoming. However, if you tend to keep more to yourself, you might not even be aware of a difference.

While you're visiting a community, make an appointment to talk with a real estate agent. The housing market, to a surprising extent, reflects the economic health of a community. Realtors have a good idea of how many new people are moving into the community each year. They also get a sense of how long they stay, based on how quickly their homes come back on the market. Remember that if you are planning to cut back on your work responsibilities, there will be more time for leisure activities. Will this be a community where you can enjoy yourself?

It's a good idea to make a short list of your basic requirements for a new community. This list should consist entirely of the non-negotiables, the quality-of-life indicators that are most important to you. It should include no more than half a dozen items. Then make a second list headed "Nice but Not Necessary." Armed with these lists, select several communities that all meet your basic requirements. Each should also have some other attractions, but don't consider them until you have verified your top priority requirements, such as cost of living.

As will be clear in the next chapter, putting together a successful job application requires a lot of work. If you first identify the places where you might really want to live, you will save a lot of time. By narrowing your job search to a reasonable number of openings, you can concentrate your energy where it will be most useful.

5   Investigating the Job Market

If you've been working for the same employer for a number of years, you may not have noticed how much the job market has changed. Not only have the jobs themselves changed, but you'll need to use different strategies for discovering them. In fact, some jobs are hidden so well that you will need to become a detective to ferret them out.

Finding Listed Jobs

Let's back up a bit, however. First you will need to find out where job openings are announced, and employers have their own rules for making such decisions. If you are looking for a job in your own field (in other words, if you have an inside track), you probably know exactly where jobs are advertised. In fact, it may be second nature to look at jobs listed on the Internet or in your professional newsletters. If, however, you are interested in exploring an entirely new career, you will need to discover the places, generally known only to insiders, where employers list their openings.

A friend has been job-hunting recently and she has reached some interesting conclusions. For example, she's found that most of the jobs advertised in the local newspaper are entry-level positions. Increasingly, online sources such as Craig's List and the Monster job board provide a better selection in urban metropolitan areas. Professional positions tend to be listed on the Websites of professional associations. Many specialized online bulletin boards list positions, and a lot of employers even post their openings to e-mail discussion lists. Less high-tech occupations are more likely to advertise in printed newsletters and journals. In other words, any given employer might advertise a position in dozens of different places. Naturally, few are willing to go to all this effort, so they choose to send their announcements to only a few.

Finding Jobs Online

Until recently, the Internet was viewed as a nice "extra" for the job-hunter, but times have changed. Online job-hunting led to more than half of the new hires in 2005, and the percentage is expected to continue to rise. Sometimes job-seekers applied online at company Websites. Other applicants found their jobs through large Websites such as Monster or CareerBuilder. In addition, the Internet facilitated many traditional ways of finding jobs, such as online classified ads. Sometimes acquaintances or a discussion groupspread the word. In fact, a number of Websites have sprung up that are devoted entirely to networking.

Classified ads in newspapers now account for only 5 percent of new hires. My friend reported that she was missing all the best jobs until she found the spots frequented by real insiders. How did she go about discovering these spots? Some of her earliest finds were the large online bulletin boards. In general, the better sites are free to job-seekers and let you contact the employer directly without having to go through the Website. She liked the ones that allowed her to see all the information about an opening without having to log in or supply personal information. As a general rule, it is not wise to give out your name, address, or phone number online, because you do not really know how the information will be used. Many sites invite you to post your resume online. Although there are some employment sites that manage to do a good job of protecting your privacy, it is usually best not to share this information unless you have read their privacy policy.

Many of the newer job sites work hard to be user-friendly. For example, T-Mobile has created a cartoon dog named Fetch, who looks for jobs that meet your criteria. Fetch will send you an e-mail if a position matching your resume comes up next week or next month. The Coca-Cola Company maintains another nice Website that has the feel of an online store. If you discover a job that looks interesting, you "Add this job to my cart." Although some sites boast many thousands of openings, my friend discovered that, in some cases, listings were not removed in a timely manner and so job-seekers might be applying for jobs that were filled weeks or even months ago. After a few false starts, she developed a useful list of favorites that she began visiting on a regular basis. Here are some of the larger and more reliable online sites:

- ☞ CareerJournal (*cj.careercast.com*). This is a large site maintained by the *Wall Street Journal*.

- ☞ True Careers (*www.truecareers.com*). This site generally provides better-than-average information about the specific job and employer.

- ☞ America's Job Bank (*www.jobsearch.org*). Nearly two million jobs are listed, so you are somewhat more likely to find what you're looking for.

- ☞ Employment Wizard (*employmentwizard.com*). This site copies job ads from more than 100 different newspapers.

- ☞ Indeed (*indeed.com*). This is actually a portal that allows you to search many different sites at the same time. It's a nice site because it shows when an ad was first posted. You can enter a zip code and find listings for jobs within a radius of 25 miles. Indeed is one of my own personal favorites, with its easy-to-scan "Google News"–like search interface.

- ☞ JobCentral (*www.jobcentral.com*). This site focuses on jobs available through member companies.

Employer Websites

If you surf to an Internet search engine and type the phrase "Job Hunting Resources" (enclosed in quotes) into the search box, you will find many other Websites that may be helpful. You are looking, however, for those special sites that are most likely to be used by employers in your occupational area. To focus your search, add a word describing your area of interest ("banking," "nursing," "retail," and so forth) after the phrase (and outside the quotes). If you are looking for a job in the corporate sector, commercial sites (their URLs usually end in "com") can be very useful. If, however, you're interested in government, education, or nonprofit organizations, then some of your best sites may be more unexpected. A good place to begin is with the online placement offices of larger colleges and universities. They may have links to professional organizations and list some of the employers who have hired their recent graduates.

As you identify useful sites, jot down their names and URLs. Compare them with one another to see which have job listings that are not duplicated elsewhere. Which seem to have the newest listings and which recycle listings from other sources?

It is also helpful to go to the Websites of employers in your area. In other words, most larger companies and government offices maintain Websites to publicize their activities, so check the "Careers," "Human Resources," or "Employment Opportunities" section. To obtain the Web addresses of these employers, you can go to any of the following directories:

- Academic360 (*www.academic360.com*). This directory takes you right to the employment pages of colleges and universities.

- BankDirectory (*www.bankdirectory.net*). This is a directory of banks, as its name implies.

- Business.com (*business.com*). This is a directory of businesses in the United States.

- ☞ USAJobs (*www.usajobs.opm.gov*). This is a job site for the federal government.
- ☞ HospitalWeb (*adams.mgh.Harvard.edu*). This is a directory of hospitals in the United States arranged by state.

Analyzing Job Ads

If you've ever been involved in hiring a new employee, you probably noticed that many of the applicants were totally unqualified for the job. You wondered why they bothered to waste their time putting an application together; it wasn't even worth the cost of the postage to mail it. No matter how specific the skills and other qualifications that are listed in a job ad, totally unqualified applicants will still apply. If you do not take yourself firmly in hand, you might find yourself among this group—those who do little but spin their wheels.

Let's suppose that you are looking for an interesting job that pays a reasonable salary. Let's also suppose that you want to do something more interesting than the kind of work you've been doing for the past 30 years. Naturally, you start by taking more interest in the classified ads in your local newspaper and you begin looking into job-hunting sites when you are surfing the Web. If you are planning to relocate, you might begin checking online newspapers that cover the geographical area where you would like to relocate.

Ads are often very brief. Sometimes it isn't even clear what type of business or industry is doing the recruiting. Remember that the managers or personnel administrators who write these ads live in worlds of their own. They imagine that their "insider" language is clear to everyone because it would be clear to their coworkers. In fact, they may deliberately choose insider terms, assuming that their language will be clear to anyone who has the right credentials for the job. As an applicant, you are in a special category. You have a lot of experience and you have developed quite a bit of expertise over the years. However, you don't really know anything about the work world outside your particular niche. Can your skills be transferred to other occupations? If so, which ones?

Avoiding the "Grass Is Greener" Syndrome

If you're feeling bored or dissatisfied with your present job, you'll find that practically every job ad sounds appealing. However, what makes them attractive has little to do with the jobs they describe. They sound interesting only because they are different. If you were hired for most of those jobs, you would quickly realize that they're no more enjoyable than your present job and you are probably not qualified for them. Those job-seekers that I just described probably suffered from this "grass is greener" syndrome. They wasted their time applying for inappropriate jobs because they were so focused on themselves and their needs. They ignored obvious clues, and saw themselves and their own qualifications in every ad.

Understanding What a Job Includes

You don't want to be tossed on the slush pile, the group of applications that are quickly passed over. Your application must, therefore, make it clear that you understand what the job involves and you have the knowledge and expertise to do it well. This means that there is no point in applying for every job that captures your interest.

Occasionally applicants will admit that they don't have the training or experience listed and then go on to say that they're sure they could learn. Such overconfidence can anger employers, especially if the missing qualifications require years of training. In fact, an HR administrator once complained that if she posted a job for a brain surgeon, some optimists would insist that they could learn the job. If you really understand the listed qualifications and believe you meet most of them, you might explain specifically how you would acquire the missing qualification. For example, you could take a particular course at the community college. If you don't really understand the qualifications listed, however, don't demean the job by assuming you can do it.

Help From the U.S. Government

To avoid wasting your time, you will need to first figure out what jobs you might possibly be qualified for. There is no better first step than to obtain a copy of the U.S. government publication *The Occupational Outlook Handbook*. This reference work, revised every two years, includes almost everything you might want to know about any occupation and is available online from the U.S. Department of Labor Website (*www.bls.gov*). It is a huge collection of information, and you may not be interested in seeing all the classifications included. Instead of viewing a huge file or purchasing the weighty volume, it may be wise to choose one or more of the specialized reprints that are available as Adobe Acrobat files (*www.bls.gov/oco/oco2008.htm*).

If, however, you would like to browse through the entire handbook, you can order your own paper copy at *www.bls.gov/emp/emppub2.htm*. It is easier to hone in on specific information with the online version, but you may find that curling up with this big book and a cup of coffee will be more helpful if you have no specific occupational area in mind. Even if you already have some ideas for a job, you may discover something totally unexpected. Most people find that they had no idea that all those occupations even existed.

Interpreting Job Titles

In almost every occupational category, there are job titles that require advanced academic degrees and sometimes even licensure. If you don't hold that degree or license, it is foolish to apply for the job. On the other hand, there are jobs that have very similar titles that do not require such specialized qualifications. The words *assistant* and *aid* are obvious tip-offs that these are not professional jobs. However, the word *technician* in a job title may have nothing to do with technical skills. Its meaning may be roughly equivalent to *assistant*. Impressive terms such as *coordinator* may also be attached to less demanding jobs. *The Occupational Outlook Handbook* makes it clear exactly what skills and education are usually required for any given job title.

If, as most of us have, you have been focused on your own job for the last 30 years, you will discover that the market is entirely different from when you were young. Both the job titles and the kind of work they involve have changed, and you will need to prepare yourself for this job market, not the one you knew way back when. Again, *The Occupational Outlook Handbook* can give you a good overall picture of the job market, and it even estimates the number of openings that will occur in each occupation. If a field is highly competitive, there may be no point in preparing yourself to enter it. If you would like to move to another city or state, it will be best to choose a job title that is readily available in many different places. Similarly, you will want to stay away from jobs that are clustered in a few geographic areas.

Analyzing the Ads

Before you become too deeply involved in the application process, spend some time taking apart the ads you find at the Websites listed in this chapter or on any of the other sites you have discovered. You will want to take notes on your computer or have pen and paper close at hand. The following steps will help to keep you on track:

- ☞ Start at the top of the list and select the first opening that sounds attractive.

- ☞ Make note of the job title and then, if it sounds unfamiliar, look it up in *The Occupational Outlook Handbook*.

- ☞ Can you find exactly the job title listed in the ad? If the answer to this question is *yes*, your work will be a lot easier. If you do not see the exact job title, you will need to match the duties and quali-fications listed in the ad to a similar job title in the *Handbook*. Let's assume, however, that you are able to find exactly the title as it is listed.

☛ Does the ad describe the duties that the person hired for this position will perform? Compare them with the duties listed in the *Handbook*. Usually, the wording in the *Handbook* will be somewhat easier to understand. Considering the two lists together, do the duties seem familiar to you? Have you done similar work in the past?

☛ Are educational requirements clearly listed, ei-ther in the advertisement or in the *Handbook*? If you don't have a required skill or degree, there's no point in wasting your time or the employer's time. If a position requires a master's degree and you only have a bachelor's, for example, then you can assume that you won't be considered unless your experience is better than the fully qualified applicants. Remember that an employer may oc-casionally waive one requirement if an applicant excels in other areas, but your qualifications have to be right on target. Your interest, sincerity, and goodwill are extras, considered only after you have overcome the initial hurdles.

☛ Find out more about the kind of duties and ex-pertise that go with this job title. In an Internet search engine, type the exact job title in quotes and the phrase "job description," also in quotes. This should produce a number of hits, hopefully actual job descriptions for positions similar to the one listed. You will probably find that some de-scribe totally different jobs with different duties. Employers may be using the job title in a way that suits their own internal needs, but it is a far cry from the way the position is described in the

Handbook. Don't allow yourself to become confused by these misleading job descriptions. Find two or three that are clearly similar to the job being advertised and print them out.

⟜ Look at the salary ranges included in the *Handbook* description and listed in the ads. If they reflect similar responsibilities, salaries should be roughly comparable to one another. Of course, salaries in large urban areas such as New York and San Francisco will be substantially higher than in small towns in Ohio, but it is not difficult to make allowances for such variation. Ideally, you are looking for a salary that is higher than a hamburger flipper at McDonald's (about $16,000–$20,000 for full-time work) or a semi-skilled office clerk ($20,000–$25,000). However, salaries greater than $35,000 usually require specialized experience. If the salary range starts at $50,000, this may not be the job for you unless you are willing to acquire some new qualifications.

⟜ When you read over all this information, can you start to imagine the person who is being sought for this position? Try to look at the position from the employer's point of view and avoid twisting it to reflect your own qualifications. Honesty and objectivity are essential.

⟜ Now compare yourself to this imaginary applicant. How are you different? How are you alike? Obviously, you have plenty of experience, but can any of it be honestly described in the same words as the qualifications listed for the job title? Are your academic qualifications at least similar to the ones listed?

⟜ Would a couple of courses at your local community college take care of the missing qualifications? Remember that if you are newly enrolled in a course, you can still mention it in your cover letter. If, however, extensive educational preparation is required, a few courses will not fool anyone.

At this point, you have enough information to decide whether a job with this title is a real possibility. You've gotten a feeling for the environment in which you would be working and you are better able to see the job from the perspective of an employer. You know now whether your qualifications are really comparable to those listed. In addition, the *Handbook* has given you a good sense of how competitive such jobs are likely to be—in other words, how many other applicants are likely to apply (based on information in *The Occupational Outlook Handbook*). Now you can make an informed decision about whether or not to submit an application.

Continue to explore job titles listed online and in your newspaper's classified ads. Repeat these steps any time you encounter an unfamiliar one. Does it sound as if this is a lot of work? When similar job openings occur in the future, you will have done your homework and be ready to make a decision. In fact, you will gradually create a list of job titles that you can quickly track with Google or another search engine. You might even sign up for an "alert" service that sends you an e-mail when a new Webpage appears on the Net. Remember that you will need to put a lot of work into developing the best possible application package and customizing it for each opening. Your research will actually save time, because you will not be tempted to apply for inappropriate positions.

Discovering Unlisted Jobs

It comes as a surprise to many of us to learn that most jobs are not actually advertised, or at least announcements are not easily discovered by outsiders. This means that much of your job search should be devoted to these hidden openings. If they're hidden, how can you expect to find them?

Even though you are an outsider, it is possible to acquire inside information, but naturally it's going to have to come from inside informants.

Identifying Employers

Begin by identifying all the potential employers in your area. If you're planning to relocate, you aren't tied down to a specific town or neighborhood so you have somewhat more freedom. Each town within your chosen location probably has a chamber of commerce, and that chamber probably has a Website. This is a somewhat tedious chore, but it's well worth going through their complete lists of members. Because there are often links from the chamber site to member Websites, you can learn quite a bit about each business, nonprofit, or other organization. Because you've already done extensive researching using *The Occupational Outlook Handbook,* you will find it a lot easier to identify potential employers, who just might have an opening that suits your needs and interests.

You might want to set up a database on your computer to hold the information you discover. Create a record for each employer that includes name, address, phone number, and the names of all the staff members and job titles you can discover. If you can find the name and phone number of the head of the human resources department or some other person closely involved in the hiring process, even better! You might also want to make note of the reason you believe this employer might have a job for you.

Meeting With HR Directors

Most sizeable organizations have at least one staff member who handles personnel or human resource matters. The responsibilities of these people, as well as the power they wield, differ from place to place, but in most cases this is a person you want to talk to. Once you have a nice long list of potential employers, begin making phone calls. Ask for the HR director if you don't know the name, but you'll have better results if you have already ferreted out both name and direct phone number. If the person answering the phone responds that there is no such person, you might ask who handles HR matters. Assume that anyone you talk to can provide useful information so be prepared with friendly (not pushy) questions. Sometimes receptionists can be surprisingly helpful, as they always know who the important people are.

If the organization boasts a bona fide HR director or personnel administrator, ask for an appointment. Explain that you will be visiting the area and would like to learn more about the organization. If you sense that administrators are on their guard, emphasize that you are not applying for a job. You just want to learn more, possibly for future reference. Communicate the impression that you respect their position and believe they're the ones best equipped to give you an overview of their organizations.

HR administrators don't usually select applicants, but they can make sure that your application gets full consideration. However, what you really want right now resembles gossip. You want an inside look at how this organization functions. Thanks again to *The Occupational Outlook Handbook*, you've done your homework and you know quite a lot about the kinds of jobs that employers such as this one might have available. Now you need specific information. First and most important, however, you want to develop a friendly, comfortable relationship that will allow you to call in the future to discuss jobs that might be available.

Meeting With Managers

Because HR administrators don't usually do the hiring, perhaps the most important information you can take away from your meeting is a list of department managers. If at all possible, you will want to arrange a meeting with any that might someday have an opening in your line. Depending on the organization, this can be quite a bit more difficult than meeting with someone in the HR department. Managers may be from the "don't call us; we'll call you" school. In general, the less pressure you put on them, the chattier they're likely to be. If you can manage to get your foot in the door, try to get them talking about their own work and their own priorities. Because of your long experience, you will readily understand the kinds of problems they face and can be more perceptive and sympathetic than a younger person. Just be careful not to do all the talking. This is not the time to impress managers with your qualifications; this will be perceived as pressuring them for a job.

Later, when you submit an application, you can remind the manager of this conversation. If you've done a good job, they'll remember a man or woman who was enthusiastic, sympathetic, and really interested in the work of the organization.

Referrals From Friends and Colleagues

Social networking is perhaps the most effective way of penetrating the hidden job market. It is most effective when you can take advantage of the many contacts you've made in your home community. Begin by reestablishing dormant relationships. Consider the men and women you know who might know about the job market. Arrange to have lunch with acquaintances you haven't seen in a long time. Become more active in the community groups in which you are a member. Consider which social and civic groups might include well-connected members. You would be amazed at the number of job openings that you might hear about while having lunch at the Rotary Club or staffing a fair booth with fellow Kiwanis members.

When you are planning to relocate, social networking becomes much more difficult. When you visit a place in which you might settle down, get to know as many people as possible. It's easy to start up a conversation with people who have an inside track to movers and shakers in a community. Make it a point to visit with one or more real estate agents. Of course, you must express an interest in local real estate, but there's no reason why you can't discuss local employers as well. Bank officers and stock brokers are also fonts of information because it's their business to know what's happening in the local economy. If you belong to civic groups that have chapters scattered around the country, be sure to attend a meeting during your visit. Make a note of the names of the members you meet and ask if you might call them with your questions.

Snowbird Savvy

Although job-hunting snowbirds will find most of these techniques useful, their situation is somewhat unique. If you'd like to enjoy the snowbird lifestyle—in other words, escape Northern winters by spending at least some of the colder months away from home—you will be faced with additional complications. Perhaps the first and most important decision you must make is whether you plan to work at just one location or find a second job for the remainder of the year. This will depend to a large extent on whether you look on the time you spend in the Sunbelt as an extended vacation. If you view these winter months as an opportunity to relax and get away from it all, then you may not want to spoil it by returning to the old grind.

On the other hand, you've probably been viewing vacations as something along the lines of the military's "R and R" (a time for recovery after hazardous duty). If you succeed in finding jobs you enjoy, then there's no need to put time aside to recover from job stress. Because loneliness can be a problem for snowbirds leaving their family and friends behind, a second job can provide a ready-made social group, among whom they'll find new friends. If they return to the same job next year and the next, then they can look forward to the pleasure of being reunited with old friends.

Some snowbirds who work in both their summer and winter communities suggest that, because variety is the spice of life, it's best to find two very different jobs. Perhaps one might be more physically demanding while the other requires more brains than brawn. Other snowbirds like the idea of two similar jobs and even prefer to work for the same employer in both places. That way, they have fewer adjustments to make each time they relocate.

An Expensive Lifestyle

While you're considering whether you need two jobs and what kind of jobs they might be, it's a good idea to consult your budget and your bank account. Earlier in the book, I stressed the importance of knowing exactly how much money you will need before you begin a job hunt. Becoming a snowbird is usually more expensive than remaining at home, even if you live simply and frugally.

Remember that you will be maintaining two homes, paying two sets of utility bills, and toting up a number of travel-related expenses. You may need to hire someone to look after each of your homes while you're away (mowing the lawn, shoveling the snow, and forwarding your mail). Look into these added costs carefully and talk to other snowbirds before making a decision. There are a number of snowbird discussion groups on the World Wide Web where members are happy to initiate novices. Yahoo (*groups.yahoo.com*) provides a home to many groups (for example, Snowbirdy, Ohio Snowbirds, and Tucson Canadians), and SeniorNet (*seniornet.org*) has an excellent discussion section ("Retirement Locations, Moving and Snowbirding").

Snowbirds Through the Eyes of Employers

Perhaps the best way to begin a snowbird job hunt is to imagine how employers will look at you. Imagine them considering your application—that is, the application of someone who plans on staying at the job for only a few months before taking off again for another part of the country. Even though it may hurt your chances, it's important to be up front about your intentions. Because you will very likely want another job next year and the next, you will quickly accumulate a stack of bad references unless you make your plans clear.

Seasonal Needs

Don't assume that an employer's reaction will be negative. After all, paying an employee to work year-round is expensive. Many occupations have seasonal peaks and valleys. These are the ones you may want to focus on. Take, for example, the tourism industry. You may not have thought of it, but you will be in Arizona or Florida or South Carolina during the height of the winter tourist season. Then you will return home just as your town, city, or state is preparing to greet its own batch of tourists. You've probably never thought about all the different jobs that come under the tourism umbrella, but there are scores of them. For example, you might want to get into resort management, convention management, tour operations, meeting planning, or the maintenance and management of recreational facilities such as parks and golf courses. Most of these jobs are either seasonal in nature or could be adapted to your snowbird calendar.

Tourism isn't the only sector of the economy that has peaks and valleys. If you are an accountant or are interested in learning to prepare income tax returns, you might be able to earn enough money during tax season to get you through the entire year. Carpenters, contractors, and other skilled tradesmen may work only during peak construction periods.

Consider, too, that when you are going South, lots of other people are doing the same thing. When you are winging your way north, you have plenty of company as well. All this means that there are more people buying at local retail stores, filling up at local gas stations, staying at hotels eating at restaurants, going to movies, and even making unanticipated visits to the hospital. Almost any industry that is affected by this influx of visitors and temporary residents will probably offer some type of seasonal employment.

You're in Demand

Because boomers are already beginning to retire, the labor market is feeling the pinch. Large retail chains such

as Home Depot are already having difficulty finding reliable customer service staff. These jobs do not pay high salaries, so they have high turnover rates and managers must
sometimes accept less-than-satisfactory applicants. Imagine,
then, a store manager looking at an experienced boomer with
a proven track record. For such employers, five or six months
may be perfectly acceptable. If he or she can also count on
an employee returning for next year's busy season, already
trained and ready to go to work, then what more could he or
she want?

Home Depot and other chains have discovered that snowbirds are among their most useful employees. They have
developed programs that allow a snowbird to transfer from
one store to another and then return to repeat the cycle. For
such large employers with retail outlets located throughout
the country, snowbirds are stable employees who arrive when
they are needed and leave when business slows down. Poli-
cies and procedures may be standardized to such an extent
that it feels to returning employees as if they've never left.
It also feels good to rejoin the friendly fellowship of staff
members.

The Right Man or Woman for the Job

Whichever type of job you choose, it's important to stand
out as someone who is especially well qualified, an applicant
who is both knowledgeable and experienced. That way, employers are getting more for their money and look at you as
a bargain rather than a liability. Few of their younger employees will arrive for work with well-established work habits and are ready to be productive staff members. You might
even want to go back to school and prepare yourself specifically for an occupation that you know offers excellent seasonal opportunities.

Ideally, you don't want to have to hunt for a job every
six months, as it is so exhausting, time-consuming, and often ego-deflating. If you enjoyed the work, it's nice to be
able to go back to the job you left last year. If you can find

just the right niche, some snowbirds say that the rest is easy. When employers discover that snowbirds are good for business, they will often hold a job until you are available and welcome you back year after year.

Becoming an Independent Contractor

Occasionally, an employer is unwilling to hire snowbirds because of the paperwork. If hiring new staff is a complicated process with lots of forms and layers of bureaucracy, he or she may be unwilling to repeat the process every six months or so. In that case, you might want to mention the possibility of becoming an independent contractor. Instead of being an employee, you would contract with the company or government agency to perform one or more specific tasks. Instead of an employer, you would have a client.

As an independent contractor, you would not be eligible for benefits, and you would have to pay your own Social Security, unemployment compensation taxes, and workmen's compensation. However, if you are eligible for COBRA or Medicare, this may not be an important consideration. It is often possible to earn considerably more money as an independent contractor than you would as an employee, so you could pay for benefits out of your own pocket. Being an independent contractor is really the same thing as running your own business. If you are a house painter, management expert, engineer, floor-layer, seamstress, researcher, writer, bookkeeper, or carpenter, you can probably stay busy and well paid by contracting out your services.

Having It All

A few lucky people are able to retire from a job, draw a pension, and continue working with their former employers as independent contractors. That way, they can set their own hours and get paid for what they accomplish, not for the time they work. Some are even able to take their work with them when they leave for their winter homes. Not every assignment can be packed up and taken with you, but there are many computer-related skills that are very portable. For example, if you can design ads, newsletters, or brochures with a desktop publishing program, you can e-mail the finished products back to the company. Computer programmers can do their work anywhere, and certain sales jobs require little more than a computer and a cell phone.

If you're interested in becoming an independent contractor, you'll need to do some research and find out exactly what the differences are between an employee and a contractor. The federal government is very fussy about this distinction, because employers have used it in the past to avoid their responsibilities. If you type the phrase "what is an independent contractor," enclosed in quotes, into a Web search engine, you will discover more than enough information.

Putting It All Together

If you have used your time wisely, you now know a lot about the job market, including the niches and crannies where your perfect job might be hiding. It is this preparation that makes this job hunt different from the others that dot your past. In the past, when you were searching for a job, you probably explored only a small fraction of the openings then available, and you considered only those jobs that you recognized as being similar to the one you were leaving. In all probability the only big difference between them was the salary.

If this is the job that is going to change your life and make it possible to really enjoy the years you have left in the workforce, then this job hunt has to be different. It must let you make a real choice, not just give in to economic necessity.

6   Fine-Tuning Your Application

Applying for a job is hard on your ego at any time, but it's especially painful after 50. You have a resume full of great experience, so why can't employers see that you're right for the job? It doesn't seem fair that you still have to jump through all those hoops, just as if you were still a 20-something greenhorn. As you've already discovered, this book starts out with some basic axioms about the job market, and one of the most important is that employers hire people who match their mental image of the perfect applicant. It just so happens that that mental picture is exactly what they see in the mirror. The supervisors and managers who do the hiring don't have time to give careful thought to each application. They look for easy-to-spot clues that an applicant is the right sort of person, and the right sort of person follows the rules. If you don't follow them, there must be something wrong.

However, the perfect applicant is very similar to the other qualified applicants for the job, only better. As you've already discovered, most of those applicants are a lot younger than you. It hasn't been that long since they were getting advice from their university placement offices and skimming through the many books on eye-catching resumes and the tricks of the trade used by successful job applicants. That means that the other application packages are similar to one another and follow certain rules.

So what are these rules that successful applicants follow? In a nutshell, the rules shape the image that you present to a potential employer, both in person and through your written materials. Your cover letter and resume are never dashed off on the spur of the moment. On no account should you drop in to pick up an application, disheveled and carelessly dressed. Apart from such basics, many of the rules are stated outright or at least hinted at in the job ad. For example, you wouldn't call for information if the advertisement states "no phone calls." Many clues are more subtle, however, and noticing and responding to them are essential parts of a successful job hunt.

The Application Package

Although parts of the package can be used again when applying for other jobs, each application should be just a little different, specifically focused on the job that is available. Of course, the next time you see this same job title in an ad, you will have most of the information you need at your fingertips. Bear in mind, however, that this is a different employer with different expectations. Look for clues in the job ad and adjust your approach accordingly.

If the next job opening you find has significantly different duties and required qualifications, you will need to make substantial changes. Later we will discuss some shortcuts that will save you time when you are applying for a number of jobs, but there are no shortcuts when it comes to research. If you don't understand what an employer is really looking for, your application is likely to end up in the slush pile.

Every application should include both a cover letter and an employment resume. Some employers also require that you complete an application form as well. Because the resume can play such an important role in determining your apparent fit for a position, we will be devoting the next chapter entirely to this topic. Some applicants toss a resume into an envelope and mail it off to an employer with no further explanation of who they are or why they are interested in the position. In other words, the resume is forced to stand on its own, naked and stripped of all the information that would help an employer see you as an individual, as someone who might fit comfortably into the organization. If you were standing before a manager or personnel administrator, you would not shove a resume in his or her face and leave. Similarly, you should never send off a resume unless it has the support of a well-written cover letter.

Writing Great Cover Letters

To be effective, a cover letter should be unique. It should say all the things a resume can't say about your fitness for *this* position and your interest in *this* employer. It is your opportunity to sell yourself to the decision-maker, and it may be the last chance you will have. Why, then, do so many people waste the opportunity? Why do so many send no cover letter at all or send a "one-size-fits-all" form letter consisting of no more than a few lines?

Honing Your Writing Skills

In some cases, the reason is that applicants do not like to write. They do not trust their ability to put together a well-written, grammatically correct letter. They imagine (with some justification) that they will be judged by their spelling and grammar. Now is a good time to decide whether this description fits you. If you have good written skills, you will have a big advantage over other applicants. If your written communication skills leave something to be desired, then there are much better ways to work around this deficiency than leaving out the cover letter.

Do you know enough about the people who will be reading your letter to anticipate their reaction? Are these readers likely to have writing skills that are much better than yours? Teachers, attorneys, and librarians, for example, are usually good writers. Business executives have probably learned to write grammatically correct sentences, but their writing may be short, direct, and to the point. Have you had experience communicating with such people? If so, you can speak their language and be somewhat less formal. However, informality, however, is no excuse for sloppy grammar or spelling. If you don't know what you are up against, it is best to take extra care with your cover letters.

Remember that the people who will be reading your cover letter will be trying to fit you into a pattern they understand. Because they have no special expertise in psychology and no crystal ball, they will be trying to discover whether the picture of you they see in your application materials resembles other people they've known who have been successful in similar jobs. In the next chapter, we'll be discussing ways to turn your resume into a snapshot of the perfect applicant. However, your cover letter provides another excellent opportunity to present yourself.

What to Include in Your Cover Letter

Because a cover letter is usually a single page, it can be hard to decide what should be included and what should be left out. The following is a list of the basic information that every good cover letter should include:

- **Begin with the job you are applying for.** First and most important, your cover letter lets the employer know the kind of position you are seeking. If you are responding to a specific ad or announcement, the exact title should be included.

- **Use your cover letter to entice your reader.** Whereas resumes are by nature "cut and dried," cover letters can actually be interesting. Think about what would interest employers and make your letter so attention-grabbing that they will want to give careful consideration to your application package.

- **Use your cover letter to add to and expand on information in the resume.** Because a letter is more "free form" than a resume, take advantage of the freedom it provides.

- **Express your personality in your cover letter.** Hint at your personality by communicating humor, success, and optimism. Describe a person who is so interesting that an employer will want to get to know you better.

- **Call attention to knowledge and skills that may get lost in a resume.** Don't simply repeat information in your resume, but showcase especially impressive or relevant accomplishments.

- **Make it clear that you can express yourself effectively.** Resumes are not always written by the applicants themselves. A unique and expressive cover letter makes it clear to the employer that you have good communication skills.

- **Use your cover letter to personalize each application.** You have limited freedom to make your resume more relevant, but your cover letter lets you respond more easily and directly to the qualifications listed in a job announcement. It's a good idea to copy some of the language in the ad or job description to catch the eye of the reader.

- **Make it clear that you've been updating your skills.** Because one of the main reasons that older applicants get passed over is the fear that their skills are outdated, so make it clear that yours are up to date. The letter must be relatively brief, so you won't be able to go into any detail, but the quick mention of an advanced computer course, trendy-sounding workshop, or high-power seminar will do wonders for demolishing an "old timer" image.

Why Do You Want the Job?

Perhaps the most important information that must be communicated in a cover letter is why you are interested in the job. This is probably not the job that you would be seeking if you were still working your way steadily up the career ladder. A younger manager may naturally assume that you have tried to take that step and failed. It is your task to convince him or her that you are not a failure and that there are perfectly understandable reasons why you are interested in this position. Don't spend time making excuses for yourself because the tone of the letter must be positive and enthusiastic. Why do you find this job exciting? Why do you think it's a perfect fit for your interests and abilities?

Remember that the reasons you provide in the cover letter should not include a need for a less-stressful or less-tiring job. You would be reinforcing the stereotype about older people lacking health and energy. However, you have other reasons that a younger person can understand and appreciate. Make a list of your real reasons for wanting the job. Then cross off the ones that hint at dissatisfaction with your present employer, stress reduction, or other reasons that don't contribute to a positive picture of both you and the position you're seeking.

What Else to Include in Your Cover Letter

Because you have had a long career, you could probably write several pages about your skills, experience, and interests. Don't! Remember that this letter should be similar to those of other applicants, but should make it clear that you are the best choice for this particular job. That means a short letter with plenty of punch. It should include just what is relevant to this particular opening. Your cover letter and your resume are your two opportunities to sell yourself before you and your materials land on the stack of rejected applications. Going through a large pile of applications is an arduous job that few people enjoy. Most try to get it over as quickly as possible. This first cut is made quickly so some very positive bits of information must stand out. Because the employer usually reads the cover letter first, it shoulders much of this responsibility.

So what should you include, and possibly more important, what should you exclude? First of all, get the name of the person to whom the letter is addressed, the address, and the job title letter perfect. Check over this information several times to be sure there are no errors. Some people couldn't care less if you misspell their names; others take umbrage at even a minor misspelling. An error in the job title alerts the reader to the possibility that this is a form letter that you have sent to other employers. Remember that you are the best applicant *for this particular job.* If you don't even know what the job is, why should the employer believe that you are the best choice?

A cover letter provides a good opportunity to "spotlight" one or possibly two of your past jobs that illustrate your qualifications. Look back into the past. Recall your most significant accomplishments. Did you receive an award, outstanding evaluation, or other commendation? Did you save your employer money or create a new procedure that saved many hours of labor? Your goal is to convince your reader that you once performed a similar job with exceptional results.

Personalizing Part of Your Cover Letter

Some job-hunters customize the first paragraph of their cover letter for each application but leave the rest of the letter unchanged. They reason that the person reading the letter will probably read only the first paragraph and will skim over the rest. This is not a bad strategy if you focus your efforts on making that first paragraph so strong that it does much of the work of the entire letter. If you use the paragraph to address the specific qualifications listed in the ad, it can be a way of using your time more effectively. Nevertheless, the "canned" section of the letter may contain wasted words that are just taking up space. If you were to rely on this information and changed only the employer, the job title, and maybe a sentence or two, you would be wasting what is possibly your one and only opportunity to make it past that first cut.

Be careful, however, that the boilerplate section of the letter is not merely a long list of all the jobs you've held. Your job history, carefully honed, is included in your resume. This is not the function of the cover letter. It is more important to present yourself as enthusiastic, successful, flexible, and quick to learn. However, simply claiming these sterling qualities is not really effective and can be somewhat annoying to the reader. Briefly tying these adjectives to accomplishments produces a stronger letter.

Tweaking the Package

When you and I were new, young arrivals to the job market, computers were still room-sized and available only to large government agencies and corporations. Job applications varied with the individual and the employer. In fact, even handwritten materials were sometimes acceptable. In recent years, personal computers, career books, and college placement counselors have brought uniformity to the application process, making one application package look superficially very similar to all the others. When one stands out, it is usually not for positive reasons. Employers, looking for quick ways to eliminate undesirable applicants, may eliminate applications that are carelessly written, smudged, or printed in a peculiar type font from consideration. Career counselors even debate the color of the paper.

This means, of course, that your application materials must be typed on a computer. Avoid sending anything handwritten or typed on a typewriter. A typewritten page has a very different look from one produced with a word-processing program. Even if you are a good typist, it will stand out and mark you as being somehow different. People who are not very familiar with computers are often impressed with the many type fonts that are available at the click of a mouse. A job application is not the place to experiment with artistic-looking fonts, and most job-hunters stick to the tried-and-true Times New Roman, or another widely used font.

Just as the type font chosen should not call unwanted attention to itself, the paper should be substantial but unobtrusive. Colors are generally undesirable, although some counselors suggest good-quality stationery in cream or pale gray to quietly call attention to your materials.

Consider Your Reader

As you write your cover letter, consider the person who will read it. Because job announcements often result in hundreds of applications, employers often ask an administrative assistant or someone else who is not really involved in the hiring process to screen the applications. This person checks to make sure that each application package contains all the pieces specified in the advertisement. In addition, the screener may check to be sure that the applicants have the basic requirements for the job. If you suspect that your application may be screened before it reaches anyone in a decision-making role, then you will want to adapt your cover letter accordingly. Your first paragraph should make clear how you meet the requirements. You will want to use almost exactly the same words as the announcement, because the screener may not know enough about the position to recognize different phrasing.

Sometimes you may decide to apply for a position even though you do not have all the required qualifications. As we discussed earlier, you should not apply unless you have some objective reasons why your qualifications are in some way equal or superior to the ones listed. A supervisor or manager might agree, but a screener is unlikely to understand such distinctions. Your challenge is, therefore, to connect your qualifications to the ones listed without playing fast and loose with the truth.

Getting Help

If you are one of those job-hunters who usually skip or copy the cover letter, you will need some help. Do you have a friend or family member who writes very well? If you are uncertain about your own grammar, it is always best to have someone else check it over for you. Computerized spelling and grammar checkers are wonderful, but there are many errors they don't catch. The best error-checkers are usually English teachers, but even your friends and family can help. Your amateur editor just needs to be good at details, observant, and able to get your corrected letter back to you quickly.

Most of us, however, are not very good proofreaders, and we tend to skip over small errors. You may find it worthwhile to hire a professional copy editor. Many Websites about creative writing maintain long lists of copy editors who work mainly with struggling writers. To find a copy editor, you might search the Editorial Freelancers Association (*www.the-efa.org*) membership directory. When I tried a search, I found the names of 530 copy editors, each with an address, phone number, and short paragraph describing their specialty areas.

As many of these copy editors are likely to be struggling themselves, they are often willing to copy edit your letters for a flat, per-page fee. (Because a cover letter is usually a single page, the cost is very reasonable.) You might work out an arrangement that allows you to attach a draft of your letter to an e-mail message. The copy editor loads the attachment on his or her computer, makes additions and corrections, and then sends the letter back to you attached to another e-mail message. If both you and your copy editor use the same word-processing program, you should have no difficulty exchanging files.

Completing Application Forms

Some employers have specially designed application forms that they require all applicants to submit. Although it is sometimes possible to substitute a resume for the form, personnel administrators often advise supervisors to insist on a completed application form. From a legal perspective, such forms make sense, because they usually require the applicant to sign a statement attesting to the accuracy of the information. By signing the statement, applicants acknowledge that employment can be terminated if any false information is provided. Another reason that personnel administrators like to use a special form is that it makes it difficult for applicants to evade difficult questions. It is usually much easier to conceal employment red flags on a resume than on an application form.

If the announcement of the job opening mentions such a form, make sure that you obtain a copy of it. Some applicants make the mistake of assuming that they need not put much effort into the form if they have all their other materials in order. Because you have no idea of the order in which your materials will be reviewed, this is definitely not a safe assumption. If a completed application form is required, you will need to put almost as much effort into it as a resume or cover letter.

First of all, how will you make the completed form look neat and professional? Many applicants simply pick up the form, sit down with an ink pen, and fill it out on the spot. However, if this is the first item a screener notices and, if it is messy and confusing, it may be consigned to the slush pile before anyone sees your carefully written resume or cover letter. Take the form home and consider carefully how you will answer each question. Most of us have sent our old Smith Corona typewriters to the dump, but libraries usually have a few typewriters for public use. If you are a reasonably good typist, this may be the best way to complete the form. If your penmanship was the delight of your high school teachers, then you may want to carefully print the information, making sure that you have correction fluid close at hand. Computer-literate applicants scan the form to their home computers and then insert borderless textboxes after each question. Many employers make their application form available on their Websites. Depending on the file format, you may be able to download the form and answer the questions using your own word-processing program.

Whichever method you choose, the application form must look almost as good as your other materials, because it has just as much chance of being noticed. Some applicants complete only the answers that are not clarified in their resumes and write or type "See Resume" beside the others. This is a somewhat risky strategy, as the two pieces may become separated or the screener or employer may not bother to "See Resume." By law, you are not required to tell your age, marital status, or certain other personal information. However, the way the application is worded may make it hard to conceal this information. You may also find it more difficult to camouflage a brief period of unemployment. In such cases, "See Resume" may be the best way to wriggle around the problem.

Online Applications

With the arrival of the Internet, the rules for sending out applications have begun to change. Many employers are using the Web to streamline the hiring process, whereas others still advertise openings and look at applications in the old-fashioned way. This can make it difficult to know how best to approach an employer.

Many corporate and government employers not only allow applicants to apply for job openings on their Websites, but they actually prefer to receive applications this way. Larger employers often use screening software programs to eliminate obviously unsuitable candidates. Let's imagine that you discover a job that interests you on a Website. You click on a link that allows you to actually apply online. Perhaps you are asked to complete an online form that contains a lot of short-answer, multiple-choice, and yes/no questions. Once you've clicked through the questions, you're then asked to attach your resume, click a button, and, presto, you're finished. Is this the best way to approach a potential employer? As with so many other questions concerning the application process, the answer is "maybe yes and maybe no."

If you're applying for a job in the computer industry, you can usually assume that the people who receive your application are very computer-literate and probably feel more comfortable with computer files than a stack of printed applications. Such high-tech managers may be accustomed to handling nearly all correspondence on their computers. What about other employers? The fear that many applicants have (and it's often justified) is that the Webmaster created the online application, but supervisors and human resource specialists are scarcely aware that the online form exists. It all depends on how computer-dependent decision-makers have become.

Take a little time to read all the information on the "Employment Opportunities" Web page. See if you can determine whether the employer actually prefers one way of receiving applications. Does it appear that applications submitted online will be considered first? Is the address to which applications should be mailed clearly evident, or is it necessary to search around the Website to find the name, title, and physical address? Employers may never actually get around to the applications that arrive in some unexpected manner.

Next, consider whether you can present yourself well in an online application. Do the questions give you an opportunity to emphasize your most positive qualifications? Do the "cut and dried" questions force you to reveal employment information that your resume and cover letter artfully disguise? Does the online application make it impossible to conceal your age? If you believe that you may not receive full consideration unless you submit an online application, you might go ahead and submit one but follow it with your regular application package. This way, you have two opportunities to make a positive impression.

It's easy to click the wrong button or make other mistakes when you are filling out an online application. If the instructions are confusing, you may feel uncomfortable and unable to think of good answers. It's therefore a good idea to print out all the questions on all the screens. Then you can take some time considering the best answers, and even write them out ahead of time. In fact, it is sometimes best to type your answers into your word processor and paste the text into the online application screen. A friend told me that if the computer program doesn't allow him to see the next screen until he has answered all the questions, he gives himself an imaginary name and types only enough information to progress to the next screen, clicking out of the Website before he must actually submit the application.

The Art of Getting to a Human Being

If an employer provides an online application, you can be reasonably sure that the same recruiting software program also screens out undesirable applications. In fact, some placement firms estimate that as many as three-quarters of all employers use some kind of screening software that allows computers to deal with obviously unacceptable applicants. That way, human decision-makers needn't waste their time doing so. Applicants also receive a response to their application almost immediately, and, if they have been eliminated from consideration, it's probably best to know the truth. However, the computer may eliminate them when a human screener might have been positively impressed with their application. Why is this the case? Why would a computer program interpret an application one way while a human being might see something completely different?

Unfortunately, computers are simply looking for patterns—a *yes* answer for a question that should be answered with a *no*, or a word or phrase that was flagged as a telltale sign of an under-qualified applicant, for example. Although the media often picture computers as super-brains, never forget that computers cannot think. Their ability to interpret what you write is very limited, so it's a good idea to consider these limitations when you submit your application. Here are some basic strategies for getting your electronic stamp of approval and sending your application on to a human being:

Create two versions of your resume. One version should be the one you print out and mail in your application package; the second version is the one you will attach to online applications. We'll be devoting a whole chapter to putting together an effective resume, and you certainly don't want all your hard work to be wasted. That recruiting software program will chew up and attempt to digest or interpret whichever resume you submit. Unless it is very simply formatted with none of the fancy flourishes that are recommended for printed resumes, the chewed-up resume may become gibberish. Avoid the resume templates that come with Microsoft Word, as they use very sophisticated formatting.

If you wonder whether the computer program will be able to correctly interpret your resume, you might try this experiment. If your resume is a Microsoft Word document, try saving it in "rich text" or "text with layout" instead. These are options that Word gives you when you select "Save as" from the menu. By closing the file and then loading the text version of your resume, you can see it more in line with the way an employer's software program sees it.

Don't use any fancy fonts in the online version of your resume; Times New Roman or Arial will work best, because they are available on almost all computers.

Use words that spell success. Use positive, assertive words when you answer online questions or submit your resume. Computer programs look for words such as *developed, managed, succeeded,* and *achieved.* Remember that the computer program has a limited vocabulary, so you can't be subtle.

Edit your resume each time you submit an online application. Repeat many of the words and phrases included in the job description. Remember that the computer is looking for certain words, and you must supply them.

Go around the computer. Make a phone call. Talk with a real person. You can always ask for more information about the job and then mention your qualifications. Even if you have to return to the online application, you'll know more about the job than you learned from the few sentences on the Website.

Develop a personal contact who works for the employer. Spend time networking at professional associations and chambers of commerce, and on other occasions when you can cultivate acquaintances who may work for the employers on your list. Friends can "let you in the back door" and can guide you past both human and computer screeners.

E-mail and Fax Applications

Both faxes and e-mails have the advantage of arriving instantly. If there is an application deadline and your package may not arrive on time, both of these methods offer a way to assure that your application will be considered. If, however, you are not struggling to get your application in under the wire, should you send it electronically? Some employers permit applicants to fax their materials or send them by e-mail. If these are options, the question is whether you should take advantage of the opportunity.

Most experts caution that you have more control over the impression you create when you send your package by snail mail (or possibly by Priority Mail or some other speedy alternative to First Class). In the end, all the application packages may be printed out and stacked together. The faxed materials are not going to look as good as the ones that were mailed or delivered personally. Applicants who fax their materials are dependent on the quality of the fax machine, the toner level, and the quality of the paper loaded in the machine (usually low-quality photocopy paper). Maybe no one noticed that the last few pages failed to print. That could mean that some of the most important information in your application is missing. Pages are more easily shuffled, and smudged ink is common. If you have to fax your package to be sure of meeting the deadline, follow it with a second package sent by traditional methods. In your cover letter, mention that you faxed an earlier copy of the materials to meet the deadline and would like to have this copy substituted for the fax. Most employers will happily make the substitution.

Similarly, the printout of an e-mailed application may be incomplete or poorly formatted. You can better control the reader's first impression with a printed application package, but be sure to consider employers' preferences. Sometimes an employer is so accustomed to communicating by e-mail that he or she has grown uncomfortable with paper. This is frequently the case with managers in high-tech industries, or it may be the preference of young managers who grew up with e-mail. (Hopefully, the job ad will make this clear by listing one address or the other.) If you sense that an e-mail submission is preferred, take as much care with it as you would a cover letter. Of course, the tone of an e-mail is somewhat less formal, but take time to compose an interesting and engaging message. Write the message offline and edit it carefully before sending it into cyberspace. Be just as careful with grammar and spelling. (Again, you may want to follow the e-mail submission with a complete paper package.)

When an e-mailed cover letter or resume is printed out, it looks much less professional than the well-formatted documents your word-processing program can produce. To get around this problem, some applicants send attachments with their e-mail message, including a resume typed into a Word file. The problem with this strategy is that many computer-savvy people refuse to open attachments, especially Word documents, unless they are personally acquainted with the sender. This is so often the way that computer viruses are spread that there is a good chance your attachment will never be opened. Again, you may have to use the e-mail option if time is short, but let the person who opens the e-mail know that the printed application package will be arriving soon. That way, he or she has the option of waiting until the package arrives, but you have technically met the deadline.

Summing It Up

In the last chapter, you put a lot of work into discovering jobs that might truly change and enhance your life. Armed with inside information on these job openings, you created an application package that stands the best chance of convincing employers that you are the best-qualified applicant for the job. However, we have not yet discussed one of the most important parts of that package: your resume. Your resume can either make or break your chances. It can present a picture of an old-timer who has held every job but the right one, or it can pinpoint exactly the experience that's needed to succeed in this particular job. Without misrepresenting their qualifications, the same applicants can totally change the impressions they make on potential employers. For this reason, the next chapter is devoted entirely to the quest for that perfect resume.

7 Repairing and Revitalizing Your Resume

If you're similar to many people, you have an employment resume filed away or saved somewhere on your computer. Whenever you apply for a job, you retrieve and update it. Updating has really meant "adding." Each time you were promoted, and each time you joined another organization or received an award, the information was added to your resume. Over time, your resume has gotten longer and longer. Now it's time to do some serious slashing and slicing. To use a cliché, what you need now is a lean, mean resume.

Describing Your Experience

Because you're tired of the old grind and looking for a job that is more satisfying and enjoyable, your present resume is probably pointing in the wrong direction. It is leading the way to a job in which you no longer have any interest. You've probably held a series of positions that progressed gradually to higher pay and more-impressive-sounding titles. When you look at your resume, you may see a career filled with hard work and success, but a potential employer takes one look and hears alarm bells going off. It just doesn't add up. The person doing the hiring thinks back to his or her own resume, and those of the other applicants hired for similar jobs. Yours doesn't fit. It stands out as a sore thumb.

Making Sense of Your Resume

You're about to change both your life and your career direction, so your resume must change, too. When younger applicants are willing to take jobs that pay less and convey less prestige than their last one, employers assume they have no choice. There must be a skeleton hidden somewhere in their closet. Years ago, my own title included the word *director*. When a new and very interesting position was created within my own organization, I applied for it and was hired. However, although the change enhanced the quality of my work life, it deprived me of that magic word *director*. My next job change was the most difficult of my entire career. Each time I applied for a job, the interviewer spotted this irregularity. Each questioned me about it, and I could tell that each deep down believed I had been asked to step down. Although there was a perfectly reasonable explanation (and my boss was more than willing to confirm it when called for a reference), I was rejected for more jobs than I care to count.

What I learned from the experience is that an employer is looking for a pattern of gradual growth and development. I learned that there are ways to be truthful, yet subtly change the impact of a resume. The secret is making judicious choices about what you include and what you leave out.

How Much Experience?

First consider how much experience you want to include. A 40-year-old generally has less than 20 years' experience. Ideally, an employee remains in the same job for three to five years, so a 40-year-old applicant might list perhaps four or five positions in the "work experience" section. Your resume should, therefore, include about this same number.

Some employment counselors advise that older applicants leave out dates entirely. This strategy allows you the most flexibility, but I have found that employers look for dates as an indication of stability. They wonder whether you have hopped from job to job, or whether you have been unemployed in between jobs. If your dates make it clear you have remained gainfully employed, it's probably a good idea to leave them in your work experience section. Instead of omitting dates, list the last 15 years or so of experience and then stop.

This will mean, however, that you should omit the dates of your academic degrees, because you would otherwise create an unexplained gap. Likewise, if the earliest job you choose to list carries an impressive title, you will probably not fool anyone. Remember that the employer is looking for a pattern of gradual progress, and anyone leaping into a position with a title such as "district manager" at the age of 25 defies belief. This strategy will only work if the title and responsibilities listed for earlier positions can, without prevarication, be made to sound relatively unimpressive.

Choosing a Resume Format That Works for You

For the man or woman who has held the same job for the past 20 years, the resume can present problems. Either your resume will make you appear qualified for only one type of work, or earlier experiences that might make you look better qualified will call attention to your age. In this case, leaving off dates entirely may be an acceptable choice. However, an even better one might be to list promotions almost as though they're separate jobs. This strategy not only provides the pattern the employer is looking for but also gives you the opportunity to list different skills and responsibilities with each promotion.

Suppose, however, that your more recent positions make you appear overqualified for the job and/or the earlier ones provide more relevant experience. Instead of starting off at the top of the first page with your most recent job, try creating a section titled "Selected Accomplishments." Make your own list consisting of all the experiences and skills you can remember, then pick and choose the ones that are most relevant to the job you have in mind. Focus not on the specific job title or dates but on the nugget that is clearly transferable to the new position. Give this section the most prominent position on the page. Remember that employers are not likely to read more than the first page of your resume before making their interview decision. Therefore, place your most positive qualifications near the top of this page.

Consider creating several resumes (one for each type of position you are considering), changing this section to draw attention to your strongest qualifications.

Age: To Fudge or Not to Fudge

Older applicants sometimes feel just a little uncomfortable tiptoeing around their age in an application. After all, the employer will discover their age if they're called for an interview. In my own experience, younger supervisors have very confused ideas about age. As you may have discovered from painful experience and possibly from the lips of your own children, 50-year-olds are sometimes considered over the hill, and 60 equates to ancient. Of course, your age will be obvious when you're interviewed. However, despite your gray hairs, you can project an image of health and vitality when you meet face to face. That's much different from the picture of tottering decrepitude that might be painted by a too-honest resume.

Seeing Yourself Through the Employer's Eyes

Age and an excess of experience are not the only clues that mark an older applicant's resume as being different. Nowadays, it is not uncommon for boomers and seniors to retire, spend a year or two deciding what they want to do with their lives, and then plunge back into the job market. Once again, this is a pattern that younger supervisors are not accustomed to. Being out of work for a year is considered a very bad sign. What's so wrong with this applicant that he or she has been unable to find employment for so long? Of course, you can make it very clear on your resume and accompanying letter that you retired, but in our age-conscious society that may be viewed as negatively as being unemployed.

In some ways, the whole point of the resume is to get you to the interview stage. Once you have made that initial cut and can actually talk with an interviewer, you will have an opportunity to explain your situation. Although, as we will discover in the interview chapter (Chapter 11), you will still need to be careful what you say in order to have a much better opportunity to present yourself in a positive light. For now, you don't want your resume to defeat you before you have had an opportunity to launch your attack. So how can you give the impression that you are gainfully employed if you haven't worked recently?

Tidying Your Employment History

Although, as I have emphasized, this is a book that advocates guerrilla tactics, recommended strategies do not include lying or misrepresentation. When you're listing recent job experience, you may wish to include the year but not the month. This can cover a period of unemployment up to a year and a half. In addition, it's likely that, over the years, you have developed hobbies or have earned money for doing work outside your regular full-time job. If you have a small home business, you can, of course, list it as a job. Successful home businesses have become so common that employers no longer see them as suspect as they once did. Computers, fax machines, and desktop publishing programs can convey the impression of a fully professional business enterprise. If you choose this strategy, it's better not to use the term *self-employed.* Instead, list the name of your business and yourself as owner.

Another commonly used strategy is listing your job title as "consultant" during the period in question. Senior employees are often asked to return to their former place of business after retirement to share knowledge or help out in a crisis (yet another reason to leave an employer on good terms). You may choose either to call this part-time employment or consulting. Too often, unemployed executives have listed themselves as consultants merely because they were available for consulting if someone happened to hire them. This has tended to give consulting a bad name among some employers. You might, therefore, wish to list yourself as a consultant to a specific company.

Occasionally, applicants cover a period of unemployment with the vague term *writer.* Once again, because this can be somewhat suspect, clarify what it is you write. A petroleum engineer who is under contract to write a technical manual about his or her subject can sound very impressive. Someone who is writing an autobiography or family history with no publisher in sight is clearly suspect. If you are thinking of listing yourself as a writer, be sure it sounds credible and that you can list some publications.

A common and quite successful strategy is to list a volunteer job in a nonprofit organization that carries a title. Nonprofits need all the help they can get, and, by becoming a volunteer, you can shore up your resume while you help to make the world a better place. This is an especially good strategy if you volunteer your services to an organization in your newly chosen career track. Again, a title other than "volunteer" is helpful. Use the opportunity to learn the language or jargon of the field so that your description of your duties will make you sound as though you're an insider. Another option is to create an unpaid "intern" position for yourself in a business organization. Again, most people are delighted to have free help and most will work with you on a title and duties.

If you took at least one course at your local community college during the period in question, you might want to list yourself as a student. In fact, it's never too late. You can enroll in a career-related course now. You will always be a more attractive applicant if you've taken relevant academic coursework. Worded carefully, your resume can make it clear that you're not unemployed but actively working toward your goal.

Women and the Job Market

Whereas most men and women of the boomer generation have too much experience, a number of women may appear to have too little. Their resumes are full of gaps and unimpressive "pick-up" jobs. For example, they might quit a job in June when their children's summer vacation begins or when the last payment has been made to the orthodontist. Some women leave the workforce for several years while their children are small and again when elderly parents need care. If you see yourself in this description, pull out your old resume and look at it as an employer might. Remember that the employer wants to see a pattern of stability and what appear to be reasonable job choices. The following suggestions are intended to produce this impression. You may wish to experiment with one or more of them, but be sure that the resume you produce is an honest one. Information can be presented in a variety of different ways, and some can be omitted entirely. Information, however, cannot be manufactured.

Remove jobs that lasted less than a year. Unless they are especially relevant to the position for which you are now applying, short-term employment that produces the impression of job-hopping nearly always works against you. How many jobs are left?

Remove the dates of employment. Because employers prefer dates, don't make this decision lightly. Does removing dates create the impression of stability and job advancement, or does it set off alarm bells?

Remove the earlier jobs. Retain approximately 15 years of recent experience. Combining these last two strategies can create a consistent pattern of steady accomplishment.

Place a "Skills" section at the top of the first page. Analyze both your paid and volunteer positions to identify the specific skills that will be useful in the new job. Experiment with wording each as a transferable skill. You've had plenty of time to acquire skills; you will be amazed at how many you can identify. You can select different skills from your list for different job openings.

Categorize your work experiences. Put similar experiences together under a single heading. This allows you to put your most relevant and responsible jobs at the top of the list. For example, you might call this first group

"Supervisory Positions," or whatever heading is most closely related to the position for which you are applying.

If you've been able to place your most impressive positions at the top of the list, add a short paragraph describing each of them. Remember that the first page of your resume is the most important. If you can catch the employer's attention with that first page, you may have earned yourself an interview, even if the next page is not as impressive.

Describing Your Education

When they get to the "Education" section of the resume, boomers have one big advantage over their younger colleagues: They've had time for many different educational experiences, including traditional higher education, workshops, seminars, individual courses, and training programs. You may never have thought of some of these opportunities as worthy of being listed on your resume, but think again. Jot down any and all learning experiences that come to mind. Of course, this long "laundry list" is not the way you want to represent yourself, but once again it gives you the opportunity to pick and choose. This is a luxury that younger applicants simply don't have. Certainly you will include your academic degrees and professional licenses. However, the other educational experiences you choose should appear relevant to the kind of position for which you are applying.

Forget the Dates

Though leaving off dates from your work history may not be advisable, feel free to do so in this "Education" section. This is such a common practice that it is unlikely that anyone will notice. If some of these experiences occurred within the last few years, however, you may want to highlight them. If, for example, you have been taking computer courses, you will want to make sure employers take note of them. Because you really can't include dates for one experience and not for the others, you will need some way of calling attention to them. A short paragraph describing them is one option. You might say, "Last year, I was fortunate to have the opportunity to attend an outstanding IT workshop. Topics covered included...." If you are going to wax poetic about a particular experience, make sure it sounds reasonably impressive. (If you are taking an introduction to word processing class, for example, you might want to refer to "computer courses," rather than identify the specific course titles.)

Other Parts of the Resume

Whereas the headings "Work Experience" and "Education" must be included in all resumes, most of the rest of the information you include is up to you. From this point on, you don't have to put anything in your resume that doesn't make you look good. Here are some of the commonly used headings:

Career Objective.	Accomplishments.
Professional Skills.	Career Highlights.
Conferences Attended.	Memberships.
Presentations.	Affiliations.
Exhibits.	Awards.
Publications.	Extracurricular Activities.
Special Skills.	Honors and Distinctions.
Language Skills.	Current Research Interests.
Computer Skills.	
Highlights of Qualifications.	References.
Personal Profile.	Honors.
Volunteer Experience.	Professional Affiliations.
Continuing Education.	Interests.
	Hobbies.

Why not take each one of these headings in turn and make a list of the items you could include? Which ones make you most resemble the perfect applicant for the job you have in mind? As we've been emphasizing, you've got to keep it short. Your resume should probably not exceed two pages unless you are in a profession in which longer ones are common. Once you have eliminated the headings that don't effectively highlight your accomplishments, what is left? Which best describe your strengths?

If you're changing occupations, you may want to put a category such as "Professional Skills" above your actual work experience. This allows you to distill the most relevant responsibilities from past jobs and highlight them in this separate section. "Personal Profile" is another heading that allows you to position your most positive points at the top of the first page. Similarly, "Accomplishments" can convey a more positive picture.

Now, which of the other headings should you include? Remember that there's a difference between bragging and selling yourself. You may have received many honors and accolades over the course of your career, but are they really relevant to the job that you're applying for? Would they make you look markedly different from the other applicants? Would they make you look overqualified? You're going to need to become comfortable with leaving out some of your more impressive qualifications. A friend of mine holds a Ph.D. from a very famous university. She had to learn that there are times when including this credential is appropriate and times when it is better left out.

Because of the widespread belief that boomers have poor computer skills, you may want to include a section with that title. Be sure, however, that you can list enough relevant skills to make the section a real selling point. If all you are able to include are Windows, word processing, and e-mail, better leave it out and sign up for some computer courses (such as Web design, business information systems, or wireless networking).

Next, decide how you will divide the space on that vitally important first page of your resume. Work experience must go someplace on that first page, because it is the section an employer looks for first. The "Education" section is required, but, unless a specific degree is required for the job or you are applying for an academic position, it can probably go anywhere you choose. So in addition to the required work history, what will you include on the first page? If you are changing occupations, it's a good idea to learn more about people who are successful in your new field. Take a good look at their newsletters and other publications to get a picture of successful managers—in other words, the kind of people who are likely to be interviewing you. (Typing an occupation name and the word "newsletter" into a search engine will produce a list of online publications. If you have friends in that field, they may receive trade journals you could take a look at, and your local library may also have some trade publications.)

What Do You Have in Common?

Once again, managers tend to hire other people similar to themselves. They may even be favorably disposed toward you if you graduated from the same university or lived in the same state. Of course, you probably do not know such personal information, but what might typically interest men and women in this occupation? What kinds of accomplishments might impress them?

Earlier in this book, we discussed tests such as the "Strong Interest Inventory" that explore how similar your interests are to those of people who work in various occupations. There is overwhelming evidence that certain personality types make similar career choices. This is true for both high-level executives and low-level grunts. It is likely that they were attracted to their jobs for similar reasons. There is, therefore, a greater likelihood that you will be happy with a job if you have a lot in common with your fellow employees. This means that even if you did not choose this occupation when you were younger, you are interested in many of the same things. Your skills and even your recreational pursuits may be very similar to theirs. If, on the other hand, you know that you are very different from people working in a field, it may not be for you. Of course, people make career choices for many reasons, but, if all those accomplishments and all those affiliations that you listed are unlike those of real people who work happily and productively in your chosen occupation, it may not be a good fit.

Finishing Touches

Once you have decided on the content of your resume, the next question that arises is: "How should it look?" Many successful businesses have been built on supplying knock-'em-dead resumes to job-hunters. They produce stylishly formatted products printed on rich, creamy, high-rag-content paper. Once you have paid the rather large bill for a few hundred copies, however, you have to use them. Each time you apply for a different job, you will adapt your cover letter to the particular opening, but you will have to include the same one-size-fits-all resume. Every component of your application package is important, but no single element is more important than your resume. Because of its skeleton-like construction, free of distracting verbiage, it is easy for an employer or screener to quickly review a pile of resumes, scanning for key qualifications. If a required qualification is listed in an ad or job description, your resume must make it clear that you have it. To limit your resume to a manageable size, you have chosen to leave out many qualifications and experiences. A few of them might be very relevant to a particular job, however, so you must have the freedom to do some tweaking. If you type your resume yourself, you will be able to make your own changes when they are needed.

Check out a career book that includes sample resumes from your local library and take a careful look at the different formats. (*Resumes for Dummies* is a good choice, as is

Resume Magic from Jist Works. Choose one of the simplest (in other words, one that does not require extensive formatting or other professional touches). Choose a format that looks clean and uncluttered. Every resume requires some special formatting. You'll want to arrange information in neat blocks, so precise spacing becomes important.

Unfortunately, word-processing programs are not quite as sophisticated as we'd like them to be, and they tend to misbehave when it comes to careful formatting. A column of information that lined up beautifully the last time you printed the page, suddenly wanders unaccountably to the left or to the right. Making small changes may cause other data to mysteriously wander out of alignment, and even an added word or two can cause the program to create a new and unwanted page. For this reason, every time you recopy your resume, you need to check it over carefully, making sure that each section is intact.

Choosing Stationery

Because it is tedious to carefully check your resume each time you print it, some job-hunters compromise by photocopying a few extra copies each time they alter their resume. If you use a good quality photocopy machine that is not running out of toner or prone to streaks and scratches, this can be a good idea. However, standard photocopy paper is not appropriate for a resume. Most "copy shacks" will allow you to use your own paper, or you can purchase better quality paper for this purpose. Business stationery conveys a professional image, so it is a good idea to order your stationery from an office supply company that carries a good line of stationery. Business executives tell me that both the too-casual photocopy and the too-elegant resume printed on the kind of paper used for wedding invitations attract negative attention. You're presenting yourself as a businessperson, so your written materials must be consistent with that image. White, cream, and pale gray stationery are all acceptable.

Because you are presenting a professional image, beware of the more imaginative type fonts. Times Roman is a frequent choice (remember: black text—no artistic brown or navy blue). Garamond adds a touch of elegance without overdoing it, but it is not a safe bet for online or e-mail resumes, as the font is not available on all computers. On the other hand, some prefer the simplicity of a modern, san-serif type such as Arial. The other 487 fonts that came with your word processor are better used with your "Yard Sale" sign or custom-designed birthday card. As mentioned in the last chapter, it's a good idea to coordinate your cover letter and resume, using the same stationery and type font.

Putting It All Together

Your resume should now present a picture of you that, in essence, says, "I'm the right applicant for the job." It shows a track record of accomplishment, and it doesn't call negative attention to you by including questionable material. It also describes the career of a stable employee who has moved up through the ranks, but plots a course toward the job for which you're applying.

Quick Fixes for an Ailing Resume

Take a good look at the resume you have put together. If you are still not sure that it can "sell" you and your qualifications, give it one last check to be sure you've made use of most of the simple quick-fix techniques listed here:

↠ **Quick Fix 1:**
Keep it short (no more than two pages). Focus on your best selling points and the absolute essentials. Leave out the rest.

↠ **Quick Fix 2:**
Include only the last 15 to 20 years. Leave out any jobs that lasted for less than a year.

↝ Quick Fix 3:

Include dates with your employment history, but leave them out in the education section. There's no need for an employer to know that you graduated from college in 1965.

↝ Quick Fix 4:

If your job history doesn't lead up to the job you're applying for, include a section titled "Skills" near the top of the first page. Because you needn't list the specific job where you acquired the skill, you can search your entire career for forgotten know-how.

↝ Quick Fix 5:

Don't include salary information. You're probably applying for a job with a lower salary than you've been accustomed to, and that's not something you want to call attention to. (Later, if you're asked about salary, you can probably skirt around it by focusing on your present salary requirements.)

↝ Quick Fix 6:

List your skills, but don't brag. If you single-handedly increased corporate profits by half a million dollars, you don't have to keep it to yourself, but surely you can compliment your team and display a little humility.

↝ Quick Fix 7:

Focus on skills that will be useful and easily understood in your new career. Stay away from industry-specific details and avoid terms that would be unfamiliar to an outsider. If you're completely changing career tracks, use *The Occupational Outlook Handbook* to translate insider jargon.

↝ Quick Fix 8:

Choose the other sections with care. Most of them are optional, so select the ones that best showcase your talents.

⇢ **Quick Fix 9:**

If the employer has an application form, treat it with care and spend time making it look good. You never know what will attract attention.

⇢ **Quick Fix 10:**

Type your resume on a computer and proofread it carefully. Refocus it for different job openings. Don't hand-write any additional information.

⇢ **Quick Fix 11:**

Have someone with good editing skills check your resume. Make sure there are no typos, formatting errors, or smudges.

That's really all there is to it. If you have "accentuated the positive," as the song goes, and "eliminated the negative," you should be well on your way to a more satisfying and rewarding job. However, putting together a resume occasionally makes you aware of weaknesses or holes in your qualifications that you never noticed before. This may be a good time to enhance your qualifications with a workshop, college courses, professional membership, or volunteer job. Just remember that this is also an opportunity to pause and congratulate yourself on all the worthwhile experiences you've had and all the expertise you've acquired over the course of your career. Never forget that you have strengths that can only be acquired with years of experience. Never sell yourself short.

8   Transforming Yourself Into the Ideal Applicant

We've all heard the adage about the optimist who sees a glass as half full and the pessimist who sees the same glass as half empty. You might want to think of employers looking at boomer job applicants in the same way. On the one hand, the older applicant may well be the best candidate for the job. He or she has plenty of experience and has had time to acquire good judgment. In fact, the boomer can bring to the job a variety of valuable experiences that a younger person just hasn't had time for. A boomer who isn't interested in climbing the corporate ladder can be more supportive of other staff members, helping to make everyone on the team a winner.

Statistically, boomers and seniors actually use less sick leave than younger employees and are less likely to hop to another job. On a more personal level, boomers have been around longer, so they know that a crisis does not necessarily mean the end of the world. They've had their share of bad times, but they can also look back on tragedies they've turned to triumphs. Many supervisors find that working with boomers tends to stabilize the group, bringing humor and a sense of perspective where others may be leaping off the deep end.

An Honest Look at Boomers

So why don't employers stand in line to hire boomers? It is true that many employers labor under inaccurate stereotypes, but maybe we should take a look at Martin. Martin is a boomer who could be a real asset to his company. He's had great experience; he has what you might call a sixth sense for spotting problems while they're still small and fixable. Martin's boss remembers times when he really saved the company's bacon, but he's reluctant to hire another boomer. In fact, it's likely that he will breathe a sigh of relief when Martin retires. The trouble is that Martin has quit trying. To start with, he both looks and acts older than his chronological age. Although he has only the usual minor ailments, he lumbers around like someone who's nearing his last breath. Because he keeps forgetting to exercise and has allowed himself to become overweight, Martin's energy level naturally flags before quitting time. Martin's sighs and groans can be heard across the office, and steering conversations away from his health is a difficult task.

Forget the Good Old Days

If you encounter Martin at the coffee pot, he'll probably tell you how the company is going to the dogs. Of course, what he really means is that things are different from what they used to be, but to Martin "different" means "worse." During the last few years, no one has heard Martin mention a single idea for the future. If you were to ask him point-blank about his own or the company's future goals, you'd discover that deep down what he really wants to do is stop change. He hasn't taken the time to really understand the current business environment or the real challenges that the future holds. That's because Martin has been coasting, imagining that what worked in the past will work in the future.

The Great Computer Divide

A computer sits on Martin's desk, and he will tell you he uses it all the time. Well, maybe not all the time, but he knows how to get his e-mail (if, that is, he remembers to check it). He's learned a few basic skills, but the computer has not changed the way Martin does his job. When Martin was younger, he knew even more about his job and his industry than most employees. He read the *Wall Street Journal* and exchanged scuttlebutt at workshops and conferences.

However, in an era when information has increased so rapidly and become such a precious commodity, Martin is completely out of step. Others quickly learn which Websites provide the best coverage for their industry. With changes occurring at lightning speed, they can't afford to miss even a week of coverage. Sure, Martin occasionally tries to do more with his computer, but it always seems to act up. He tries, and what happens? It crashes, or even worse, gets infected with a virus. Then the young smart-aleck technician gets all huffy; it's easier just to work around it.

When Martin was young, he knew that success depended on learning the ropes. When he realized that he had a weakness, he did what was necessary to make himself more marketable and more successful. At some point, however, he stopped learning. Maybe the job no longer interested him. Maybe he thought he knew everything there was to know. Now Martin is five or maybe 10 years behind. When he gives advice to younger employees, they can easily see that he's using yesterday's information and yesterday's vocabulary. Even though deep down there's often a kernel of wisdom that they would do well to heed, it may be all but impossible to discover it.

Do You Recognize Martin?

I'm sure you're getting tired of hearing about Martin. It's especially uncomfortable because there's a little Martin in all of us. As I get older, I find that I have more sympathy with the Martins of the world. They often have reason to be disgruntled, and it's true that to some extent they are misunderstood and under-appreciated.

Martin is a loser, however. The years before he retires will be unhappy ones, and it is unlikely that he will find more meaningful pursuits in retirement because of the bad habits he is accumulating. Happiness depends, in large part, on accepting the world as it is. Martin's desire to stop the world and let him get off will bring him nothing but unhappiness. Although occasionally plunging into the past can be a delightful hobby, real life is even better.

Seeing Yourself as Others See You

If Martin decides to apply for a new job, it's easy to predict what will happen. Martin may think he's the victim of age discrimination, but let's be honest: Why would anyone want to work with Martin? At this point in his life, Martin may be beyond help. His gloomy outlook and bad habits are too firmly entrenched. Most people, however, just need to be able to see themselves as others see them. Although you are who you are, you can change your more destructive habits and reap huge benefits. To know which habits need changing, it's important to consider the image you project. Step away and look at yourself objectively as your colleagues see you.

First Impressions

So how do you appear to the people you work with? Let's imagine that you've come to apply for a job. The camera's rolling so you'll be able to see yourself as the camera sees you. Later on we'll fast-forward our imaginary camera to watch you as a new employee being looked over by your new colleagues. As you know, it's hard to forget a first impression, and first impressions are made up mainly of very superficial things. A first impression includes the way you look, the way you walk, the way you smile, and the way you speak. So let's start there. Let's begin with that first quick impression.

Greetings. Okay, you've announced yourself to a secretary or receptionist and you're being escorted into the interviewer's office. I hate to keep saying "he or she," so this time we'll make our interviewer a woman. Next time, it will be a man. You're walking into the office and she comes around her desk to shake hands. Is your handshake enthusiastic or limp? Are you smiling warmly and making eye contact? Do you have something prepared to say during these first uncomfortable moments besides "nice to meet you"?

Beware the chair. Now she's inviting you to sit down. Most of us cannot rise gracefully from a squashy lounge chair without difficulty. If you're given a choice, select the harder, firmer chair. Don't, however, make an issue of it. Now is not the time to mention your arthritis or bad back.

Appalling apparel. What are you wearing? Did you purchase most of your work clothes more than five years ago? Queen Elizabeth may be able to keep her job and continue to dress as she did in the '50s, but most of us are not that fortunate. I had a good friend who told me one of his goals was to wear out his wardrobe before he retired. He had spent a lot of money on those suits and sports jackets, and he was sure as heck not going to waste money buying more. Saving money is a good thing, but this is definitely overdoing it.

If your clothes make you look different from your colleagues, you haven't been keeping up with the times. Typically, people pay a lot of attention to their wardrobes in their 20s and 30s. As time goes by, clothes become less important. Eventually, your wardrobe may become one of your lowest priorities. However, when colleagues at work look at you, your costume is a big part of the picture. If you're a woman wearing a polyester double-knit pantsuit and everyone else is wearing outfits purchased within the last couple of years, then you will stand out like a sore thumb.

Many workplaces have become less formal. Look around you. If you are the only one still wearing a dress, tie, or high heels, then you are making yourself appear different and consequently old-fashioned. Casual, however, may not mean what you think it does. In fact, the phrases *workplace casual* and *dress-down Friday* refer to specific styles of which you may be unaware. Many complain that it is actually harder to create a crisp, professional look when one can no longer depend on tried-and-true business suits.

As we get older, we want comfort in our clothing and, even more importantly, in our shoes. We tend to choose elastic waists, rubber soles, and loose garments that don't bind or pinch. There's nothing necessarily wrong with this. To some extent, younger people do the same thing. However, it's easy to develop a look that reminds younger people of their grandparents.

If you're not usually aware of fashion trends, take a good look around you. Observe the smart-looking men and women in your office—not the trendy teens, but people in their 30s and 40s. What do they wear to work? Where would you place their wardrobes along the spectrum from formal to casual? Would you be likely to wear a similar jacket or pair of slacks? How wide are their ties and lapels? How long are the women's skirts? You have probably heard it said that anything goes nowadays, but that's not really true. There is more variety, certainly, and you don't see nearly identical outfits. However, people with some fashion sense can spot out-of-date garments from afar, and they make assumptions about the person wearing them.

You may find it helpful to spend some time in clothing stores and request mail-order clothing catalogs. Both stores and mail-order companies market their merchandise to specific customer groups, so be sure they're aiming at businesspeople, not at retirees or 17-year-olds. When you've accumulated a collection of catalogs or when you're visiting the local mall, analyze individual articles of clothing. I mentioned lapels, skirt length, and tie width earlier. What about colors? Nothing can date an outfit quicker than a color that everyone was wearing five years ago. What about pleats and cuffs? Are pants form-fitting or baggy? Are women's sleeves puffed at the shoulder or smoothly tailored?

Dated hairstyles. Let's return, however, to the image that you're projecting and the way it is interpreted by the interviewer. How long have you been wearing your present hairstyle? Another way to approach this question is to ask the age of your barber or hairdresser. Hairstyles date people just as much as clothing does. If you are a woman who is still wearing one of the puffy hairstyles of the 1970s, you're out of step with the times. If your barber is older than you are and he's been cutting your hair the same way for the last 20 years, then you're ready for a change.

So granted that your hairstyle is out of date, how do you go about changing it without making yourself look ridiculous? After all, you've probably left it unchanged all these years because, after a number of embarrassing experiments, you finally found something that suited you. If you're a man, your problem is not so very difficult. Ask a younger person (not a teenager) to recommend a hairstylist and request a contemporary but conservative cut. Notice that I did not use the word *barber.* Although there are barbershops that have changed with the times, most have not, and you may be safer entrusting your hair to an establishment that advertises "unisex hairstyling."

If you're a woman, it seems to me your job is a more difficult one. You too probably need a younger stylist but most young women are wearing long hair now. Such styles just aren't complimentary to older women. You will first need to identify a stylish shorter hairstyle, possibly one found in a magazine. Fortunately, today's hairstyles are a lot simpler to manage than yesterday's, and a blow dryer may be all you need to keep yours in shape.

Check your scale. Contemporary society is not only weight-conscious, but you might call it weight-obsessed. Prejudice against obese persons is rampant. Employers may not often speak of it, but there are certain unpleasant assumptions that come to mind when they meet someone who is overweight. Most of these prejudices (such as assuming an overweight person is lazy or slothful) have little basis in fact. However, when they see large men and women puffing their way up a flight of stairs, they can reasonably infer that their energy level cannot compare with that of a slimmer person.

Whether prejudices are founded in fact or not, there is ample evidence that overweight people have more trouble getting hired and promoted than slimmer people. Many studies confirm that looks matter and weight is the most important single consideration when it comes to assessing attractiveness. As we get older, it becomes more difficult to lose weight. For all but a few of us, however, it continues to be possible to do so. In fact, by keeping our weight under control, we reduce the chance of heart disease, stroke, and many other debilitating conditions. That means it's well worth the effort. More than 60 years ago the Metropolitan Life Insurance Company introduced its standard height-weight tables for men and women. In 1983, the tables were revised based on new medical knowledge. It's easy to find them online (go to Halls Health Calculators and Charts [*www.halls.md / ideal-weight / met.htm*] or Blue Cross [*www.bcbst.com / MPManual / HW.htm*]), or you might ask your doctor to suggest an ideal weight to shoot for.

Don't Overdo It

Apart from these basic changes, how much effort should you put into looking younger? Should you dye your hair? Should you use more makeup or invest in cosmetic surgery? Job counselors differ on these points. In general, however, you should apply a policy of moderation to any changes you make in your appearance. For example, dying white hair black may produce an unnatural look that will make you look older rather than younger. However, a shade of ash brown might go unnoticed.

As I write, I am thinking of a woman of 70 who continues to dye her hair red. Actually, it comes out an ugly shade of orange with white roots that give her a somewhat comical look. On the other hand, I met the famous actress Greer Garson when she was in her 80s. It was clear that the famous redhead was dying her hair, but it was a lovely, soft shade, almost an apricot, which complimented her lined but still beautiful face. It was obvious that Greer did not depend on do-it-yourself hair dye purchased at a local drug store. This made me realize that hair dye is an expensive, ongoing commitment and, if you can't afford to have it done professionally, maybe you're better off with glossy, well-styled gray.

Women also ask about makeup. My own feeling is that some makeup is essential and modern age-minimizing foundations can do wonders for wrinkles. However, heavy eye make-up usually tends to make women resemble an aging madam or the Witch of the West.

After the First Impression

Now let's imagine you've passed your "first impression" test with flying colors and you're talking with the interviewer. Remember: Our camera is rolling, so we'll be able to observe your part in the conversation.

Are you doing all the talking? Bad sign! In this situation, as in many others, listening is a more useful skill than talking. Of course, a potential employer wants to know about your experience but not at interminable length. What she really wants to know is whether you'll fit into the organization. Unless you ask good questions and listen carefully to the answers, you won't know what she's looking for. You'll be making assumptions about what you think she wants and you may be totally off the mark. Remember that you don't need to describe every work experience you've ever had. Younger people don't have a similar list, and they're the people you're competing with. Talking too much can make it all too clear that you've been around for a long, long time.

Your On-the-Job Image

Let's fast-forward our camera to your first day on the job. Let's assume that you managed to acquit yourself credibly at the interview and you are now a probationary employee.

Some job applicants have become experts at the interview process. They have special interview wardrobes and even special interview personalities. In other words, they have learned exactly how to behave in an interview. However, the person they bring to work with them is altogether different. Once the job has been fought for and won, the pressure is off. The interview outfit goes back into the closet and out comes that same disenchanted, ill-dressed employee who fled from the last job.

Computers Aren't Decoration

What, for example, are you going to do with that computer sitting on your new desk? If you were wise, you came prepared for this moment. You have been practicing your computer skills, even signing up for evening classes at your local community college. There is no single passport to a new and more rewarding career that works as well as real computer skills. By that, I don't mean that you can read your e-mail or check the Dow Jones average on the Web.

In general, it's best for boomers to learn computer skills off the job. Even when an employer provides computer workshops, boomers are usually at a disadvantage. That's because we lack the amazing eye-hand coordination we see in our grandchildren. Thanks to those computer games they grow up with, a computer mouse is almost a third hand. It's very unlikely that you will look good when you're struggling just to manipulate the cursor. If you put the time and effort into it, you'll probably discover that you can become just as skilled at most computer programs as younger people. However, if you didn't grow up playing "Tomb Raider," that eye-hand part will always be a struggle.

Catch That Memory

While we're on the subject of brain peculiarities, it might be a good idea to get that camera rolling again while you attend your first staff meeting. Do you notice how that young fellow across the table is reeling off facts and figures without even looking at his notes? He has no trouble remembering names, dates, or other particulars. What he's demonstrating is a great short-term memory. If you're feeling intimidated, you're not alone. Your short-term memory is not what it used to be, and most boomers are experiencing the same problem.

If a fact is right on the tip of your tongue, if you sometimes forget the names of people you work with every day, if you even occasionally forget your own telephone number, then you're in good company. Most of your fellow boomers report the same frustrations. No, it doesn't mean that you're getting Alzheimer's disease or that senility is right around the corner. Your brain is still ticking along efficiently just as it always did, but you're going to have to find ways around your unreliable memory.

Memory Tips and Techniques

We all have problems with short-term memory, and they get more annoying as we age. There are, however, some useful tricks to minimize the problem and there are even ways to actually pep up those memory cells a bit. Because our camera is rolling, let's go back to that staff meeting. At your elbow are your notes. You have anticipated the information that you will need to participate fully in the meeting. In fact, you've probably spent more time preparing for the meeting than your younger colleagues. You have long years of experience with meetings and you can use that knowledge as you get ready.

One acquaintance of mine decided that he would stop worrying and get his unreliable memory under control once and for all. Henry is never without the pen and small memo pad that he keeps in his pocket. He also uses a larger pad to take meticulous notes when he attends meetings. What he is looking for are snippets of information that may be useful to him in the future. He's not trying to be a secretary recording the entire content of the meeting. Instead, he's jotting down facts and figures that may prove useful. He does the same thing when he surfs the World Wide Web at home. However, this information is of little use until he organizes it.

Computer to the Rescue

As a way of developing his computer skills, Henry transfers information into a simple database, possibly created in Microsoft Access or Microsoft Works. He makes a record for each person he meets or hears discussed. He includes their full name, their duties, and anything else he learns about them. Because some of these people are customers, he focuses on their interests and how he might best approach them. Sometimes he even pastes sections of e-mail messages into the record, just so he has all the information he needs about an individual in one place.

Henry also uses his word-processing program to keep him from forgetting important information. Each project he's working on has what he calls a scribble sheet. This is a single word-processing document into which he "dumps" his own ideas and the information he gets from his boss and his colleagues, as well as his own research. When he needs to produce a report, he never has to start from scratch and has most of the information he needs at his fingertips. When he meets with his boss to discuss the project, he uses the scribble sheet to make an outline of the points he plans to make.

Rev Up Those Gray Cells

I mentioned that there are ways to actually pep up your tired memory cells. Ginkgo biloba, for example, is a dietary supplement that typically comes as an extract made from leaves of the Ginkgo biloba tree and contains something called phytochemicals. There appears to be good evidence that it works well for normal age-related memory loss, Ginkgo has been well documented to improve cerebral blood flow and to reduce the age-related decline of neurotransmitters and receptors. Long-term use of vitamins A, E, and C also appear to improve the memory, slowing vascular degeneration, and improving brain function. B vitamins also appear to be useful for memory and brain function. Many memory stimulants depend for their effectiveness on antioxidants that protect the central nervous system from oxygen damage. Another example of an antioxidant that's been in the news recently is evening primrose oil or seed. None of these are magic bullets that will restore lost memory, but they may provide the extra jog you need to remember the name of the woman who works in the next office.

Of course, memory stimulants will not help you if you simply don't have the information to begin with. How much work-related reading do you usually do? What newsletters and Websites do you read on a regular basis? Let's go back once again to your first staff meeting. Staff members who appear to best advantage are usually the best read. They keep up with what's going on in their industry and are the first to know of new trends.

Spending Your Time Wisely

Although some of this reading may be done during working hours, much of it is done at home. Are you interested enough in the job to devote time at home to reading and research? In the first chapter, you gave a lot of thought to what you really wanted to do with your life. One of the reasons that many boomers give for changing jobs or career paths is simply that they're not interested in their work. They're not willing to give it the extra attention the job demand. If you're in banking, for example, how do you feel about reading and thinking about banking during the hours when you're "off the clock"? Do you resent any extra time spent boning up? If your answer is *yes*, you may want to rethink your chosen occupation. When we get to our ripe old age, we have a right to enjoy our work. If you don't, there are usually other options available to you.

Although we touched on ways computers can make you more successful in your new job, there's a lot more you can do with your computer. In fact, improving your computer skills may be the key to solving many of the problems that boomers face in the job market. For this reason, we'll be devoting the next chapter entirely to computers. Don't get nervous, however. Even when it comes to these newfangled machines, you have talents that younger employees will have to wait years to acquire. When you expand and enrich those skills with computer skills, you become a powerhouse that's hard to beat.

9 Computer Basics for the Job-Hunter

Following the tragically inadequate response to Hurricane Katrina, a Congressional investigation revealed that many agencies and individuals were at fault. One unexpected finding, however, was that the two members of President Bush's Cabinet most centrally involved with disaster planning, both over the age of 50, never checked their e-mail. (In fact, testimony indicated that these two Cabinet members did not regularly use e-mail at all.) Other high-level administrators also failed to read their incoming e-mail messages, and therefore were unprepared to take action when action was needed. It would be unfair to assume that age was the source of the problem, but the investigation revealed that younger staff members were much more likely to communicate information via e-mail. This became especially important when telephone lines became jammed and all but unusable.

For almost the first time in human history, it was possible to instantly send vital information to a dozen or more key relief offices and agencies. Overworked administrators, struggling to cope with the many demands on their time, could at least communicate with their superiors, their subordinates, and their colleagues in other agencies by sending up-to-the-minute information in a single e-mail message. The Congressional inquiry made it clear, however, that in many cases, these essential updates were ignored. Many decision-makers lacked the accurate information that was needed to act effectively, even though that information was waiting on their desktop computers.

The Communication Revolution

The report that included these findings did not go into detail about the government's use of e-mail, but there are millions of offices across the country where you can see exactly the same problem. People younger than 40 tend to use e-mail for most of their correspondence. Many run sizeable businesses from far-flung locations almost entirely by e-mail. If you are even a minimally adequate typist, you can whip out a message in five minutes that will zip through cyberspace in seconds. The same information included in a memo or typed on letterhead stationery would require about half an hour to type, print, sign, fold, and seal. It would have to wait until someone collected the mail and require at least a day to arrive at its destination if sent by overnight mail. A telephone call is immediate, but it depends on the person at the other end of the line being available when the call comes in, something that is rarely true during a crisis. Of course, the recipient might not be immediately available to read an e-mail message, but it would still be, generally speaking, considerably faster than a letter and more reliable than a telephone call.

It is no wonder that younger people have turned to e-mail. However, it requires a computer and a computer-literate reader at the other end. It is not just in government that older administrators fail to seize opportunities because they are not really comfortable with computers. This gulf between older and younger workers exists in nearly every business and nonprofit, every educational and cultural organization. Computers are not simply a new type of business machine, such as an extra-efficient typewriter or high-speed adding machine. They have revolutionized the way business is conducted. It is no longer possible to work around them and still function effectively.

"Oh, I know how to use e-mail," one of those administrators might have said. "I know how to bring up the program and click on the message." You may be among those who have learned enough to press the right keys—but computers have not become part of your life. E-mail is a good example. The effective use of e-mail means checking for incoming mail several times a day. It means controlling the amount of mail you receive by filtering out spam and organizing the remaining messages. It means moving messages out of the Inbox so that new ones are not lost among dozens or even hundreds of other messages. It means identifying incoming viruses before they can contaminate your computer and those of everyone in your address book.

Boomers and Computers

One of the biggest obstacles you will encounter in your job hunt is the assumption that boomers lack computer skills. Although you would like to say that this is yet another erroneous stereotype, it is all too often true. If you challenged some employers about this assumption, they could probably point to numerous examples of older employees who never became skilled enough with computers to be really productive. In some cases, their errors cost their companies thousands of dollars.

In general, employers do not believe they should be responsible for basic computer training. White-collar workers have come to expect computers on every desk, but boomers often find ways to cut computer use to the bare bones. Most have learned to send e-mail messages and to perform other simple tasks. Instead of learning computer basics, however, they memorize certain routines, pressing certain keys and clicking their mouse cursors on certain options. They can do little more than go through the motions. They may forget to back up their data, causing hours, days, or weeks of work to be lost. They may not really understand computer viruses and may crash an entire network by failing to update their anti-virus program or opening an obviously suspect e-mail attachment.

The Technology Generation Gap

Of course, this is not true of all boomers, and many young people are just as clueless. However, it's so often an accurate picture that you're going to have to work hard to convince an employer that you are just as computer literate as younger staff. Your younger-than-40 coworkers, however, grew up with computers. Even at the age of 4 or 5, they learned their numbers using an animated software program hosted by Barney the Dinosaur or Winnie the Pooh. They spent so much time with a computer that they learned to deal with problems as they occurred. Gradually, as they got older, they turned to their computers to perform everyday tasks, and each problem they solved made them more skillful and confident.

There's probably no way for you to achieve this skill level without some kind of formal training (ideally, courses at your local community college). If, however, you do not own a home computer, the skills you learn in the classroom will never become second nature. If you're very disciplined, it is sometimes possible to schedule an hour or two a day on a computer at your local public library or senior center. There is usually a staff member on duty to assist you. Though this can be very helpful, there's always the temptation to let the staff member do the work for you. When you encounter a problem, you simply call for help. This is fine when you're just starting out, but no employer will be willing to "hold your hand" on the job. The sooner you can work independently, the better.

Testing Your Computer Skills

As you read about other boomers with weak computer skills, you may not be sure whether or not you fit the description. Yes, you use a computer, but how do you use it? Perhaps the best way to assess your own computer literacy is to think about the last project that you were assigned. As you planned the way you would go about it, was the computer a big part of your planning? Did you think about how you would gather more information using the World Wide Web? Did you consider asking for suggestions from your e-mail discussion list? Did you think about a spreadsheet or database that would help you organize your information? When it was time to update your coworkers on your progress, did you use a presentation software program? In other words, did you think of the computer as an essential tool and put it to work on your project without prodding from others?

This might also be a good time to have a heart-to-heart talk with yourself. Many people find it hard to examine their skills, because that would mean knowing what they don't know. However, it's a lot easier to take a good look at your feelings. For example, would you describe yourself as being uncomfortable with computers? When your computer misbehaves, do you blame the computer or set about fixing the problem? Have you ever felt a wave of panic come over you when colleagues were talking about the work they did on their computers? Did your anxiety level rise because you wondered if, just possibly, the whole world had left you behind? If matters have really gotten out of hand, it's even possible that deep down you believe that you are too old and too inept to learn.

If you've purchased a home computer, does it sit gathering dust in your recreation room or den? Maybe you've decided that some mysterious chip or neuron that's implanted in younger people is missing from your brain. As you watch your 10-year-old grandson playing "Tomb Raider" or some other equally mindless computer game that requires extraordinary hand-eye coordination, your conviction may grow that this is not the machine for you.

Setting Realistic Goals

In one sense, you are right. You will probably never be able to play "Cosmic Invader" with the same skill as an adolescent. What you may be forgetting, however, is that you wouldn't want to. The years have made you into a far more sophisticated person who demands more in the way of mental stimulation than such games have to offer. Fortunately, there is more to computers than zapping 1,342,686 alien invaders. Computers can help you pursue almost any personal interest and can even make it possible for you to achieve your goals. Such adult activities involve little hand-eye coordination, but they do require skills and experiences that you have acquired over the course of an active personal and professional life. As with most rewarding adult activities, they require thought, not speed, so you're already well on your way to becoming a first-rate computer user.

Organizing Your Job Hunt on the Computer

A computer is possibly the most useful tool you can have when you're looking for a job. Because it is essential to develop good computer skills to compete in the job market, begin immediately to use the computer to help you make decisions about your future. As you have already figured out, there's really no way to learn how to use a computer without having one close at hand. Your easiest access is, of course, your office computer, but, as mentioned, work is not a good place to display your inexperience. If you don't feel ready to purchase your own computer, your local senior center or library is a good place to explore leisure pursuits on the World Wide Web.

Getting Help

If your confidence is at low ebb, it will be helpful to have a helper, someone who can rescue you when you need rescuing, reset the computer, and get you back on track. A family member such as your grandson is not the best person to look to for help. He will very likely begin by telling you, "it's real easy," and then punch dozens of keys in rapid succession, while you sit by feeling helpless and utterly confused. An instructor or volunteer at your senior center is experienced in teaching beginners and is more likely to remember all those little steps that have become second nature to your grandson. Another adult is more likely to remember that, when you're starting out, these steps must be learned slowly and painfully. If you've already progressed beyond very basic applications, courses at your local community college will also provide a readily available computer lab and an instructor who can answer your questions.

In earlier chapters, you considered a variety of options including retiring, choosing a new job, possibly in a new location, or even starting your own business. To make such an important decision, you need all the information you can get. No place compares with the World Wide Web when it comes to finding facts. Because Web browsers are the most common and easy to use computer programs, you probably have some experience surfing the Web. You may not, however, have been looking for the kind of specific information that will help you make these important choices. Make a list of the questions you have about each of your choices. Some examples follow. Your own personal questions will, of course, be different. Then select either the Google or Yahoo search engine.

Cost of living. If you are considering moving to a new area, you will want to know how the cost of living there compares to the cost of living in your hometown. In the search engine's "Basic Search" box, type the words "cost of living" enclosed in quotation marks. Note that quotation marks are an important requirement in a good search. They force the search engine to look only for those words in precisely that order. Outside the quotation marks, type the city and/or state you are interested in. Some of the "hits" that the search engine retrieves may include comparisons of the cost of living in a number of different places. Your hometown may be listed or you may need to do a second search, substituting your hometown for the one you searched.

You may want to perform a similar search on housing costs. In this case, you would enclose the phrase "housing cost" in quotation marks and add the appropriate city. An even better way to compare housing costs, however, is to go to the Websites of Realtors in the area you are considering. Then you can compare actual houses that are currently for sale with houses listed on similar sites in your hometown.

Job listings. There are essentially two ways to look for a job on the Internet. The first is by occupational area, and the second is by location. It is often possible to combine the two on the larger Websites. Because there are thousands and thousands of Websites that list job openings, you will probably be finding new ones throughout your search. Right now, go to *www.monster.com.* This is a large site that lists a huge number of job openings. Another very large site is *www.craigslist.org.* Websites such as these often ask you to sign up or log in to see the listings. They may ask you for a variety of personal information. For the time being, do not give out any personal information. Large job sites such as these are rife with scams. Cyber-criminals invite you to become their U.S. representative acting for illicit, offshore companies; others promise $100,000 your first year. These are definitely not people who should have access to your personal information. If a site does not allow you to see its listings without going through a sign-up procedure, invent the information. Later, you will find that it is in your own interest to occasionally provide personal information, but for now make it a rule that you will keep info such as your home and business addresses, personal e-mail address, and telephone number confidential. It is a good idea to create a free e-mail account on a service such as Hotmail or Yahoo so that you can give out that e-mail address when necessary. Don't use that address for your personal correspondence.

The classified advertisements in your local newspaper are also online, so checking them on a regular basis should become a regular part of your day. Again, keep personal information confidential. Some people find it helpful to create a sort of imaginary friend. When they are asked for personal information, they give the same name, birth date, e-mail address, and home address, all of which are imaginary.

Financial information. To make the right decision, you will need to know how much money you have and how much you will need to achieve your goals. An excellent way to see how you presently spend your money is to log into your bank's Website several times a week. You can see exactly how much money is in each of your accounts, and you can easily keep track of daily, weekly, and monthly expenditures. Financial information, however, is highly confidential and should not be viewed on a public or workplace computer. To see your account information, you will need to provide your Social Security number and other highly confidential information that could easily be misused. Identity theft has become all too common in recent years, and your Social Security number in the wrong hands can set you up to become a victim of crime. To check your bank account, pension earnings, or investments online, you will need to purchase your own computer. In addition, you will need to become familiar with anti-virus and anti-spy software programs to prevent intruders from gaining access to your computer.

Credit cards and public computers. Online shopping is one of the most popular uses of the Internet. Even if you are not a proficient computer user, you may feel tempted to purchase Christmas or birthday presents online to avoid the hassle of crowded stores and unpleasant clerks. However, online shopping involves using your credit card number to purchase merchandise. If you use your home computer for shopping, be sure that your anti-virus and anti-spyware programs are up-to-date before entering credit card information. Before you enter your credit card information, check the bottom of the screen for the small gold lock that identifies a secure site. The possibility of identity theft is too great to entrust this information to a public or workplace computer. It is not uncommon for hackers in public computer labs to load programs that remain memory-resident, keeping track of every key you and other users type. The hacker can return later and copy this information.

If you don't own a computer, you can still take advantage of interesting Websites, but more caution is in order. For example, you can check airline fares or hotel amenities online and then call the toll-free number listed on the Website. Later, when you have your own computer, you can actually make your reservations online.

Keeping Track of Important Information

Almost every Windows-based PC comes with the Microsoft Outlook program. If you are currently using e-mail, you may already be familiar with the e-mail module of this program. More likely, however, you are using the stripped down Outlook Express. Full-featured Outlook includes several modules that can help you organize your job hunt and use your time more effectively. You will probably find the program listed on your computer's "Start" menu. When you load it, you will be asked a number of questions so that the program can be set up for your personal needs. This is not information that should ever reside on a public computer; Outlook is really intended for use at home.

A more useful address book. Why not start with the Contacts module. This is really just a super-efficient address book, but, as your job hunt progresses, you are going to have a lot of contacts to keep track of. The big advantage of this computerized address book is that it provides room for your notes. Not only can you include the usual information, but you can actually keep track of the letters you have sent and the phone calls you have made. If you learn more about an employer while you are searching the World Wide Web, you can simply copy and paste this information into Outlook's "Note" field.

Your calendar. Outlook provides a date book very similar to the printed executive models that often cost an arm and a leg. What makes the computer version better is the way it can expand and contract. You can add as much information as you need. For example, if you have a telephone interview scheduled, you have space in your calendar to list the names and job titles of all participants and any other information that will be helpful. Outlook can also alert you in advance to an appointment, but you have to get into the habit of loading the program every day.

To-do list. It is easy to set up your to-do list for each day. However, be sure to check off items when they're completed. Outlook excels at nagging. A friend recently enlightened me about Yahoo's widgets. These are small programs that are displayed on your desktop whenever your computer is turned on. There are several "To-Do List" widgets; the one I like best is called "What to Do." It's simply a brief list that sits on your desktop silently nagging you to get to work. Some people want to be nagged, whereas others prefer a different approach. One of the best reasons to become more comfortable with your computer is your ability to tweak it, making it compatible with your own personal work habits.

Choosing a Word Processor

Once you become aware of a job opening and investigate it thoroughly on the World Wide Web, you will want to send out a letter expressing interest in the position. This means that you will need to become reasonably good at using a word-processing program. At present, the most popular program is Microsoft Word. However, there are several other very satisfactory programs on the market including WordPerfect. As long as you will be printing out your letters and resumes, it doesn't really matter which program you use as long as you are happy with it. If you will be attaching your resume file to e-mail messages, however, you will need a program that the person receiving the e-mail message is likely to own. Most programs can convert text from other programs, but a resume is so carefully formatted that it is unlikely to come through the conversion process looking the way you sent it. If you think you will be e-mailing your resume on a regular basis, Microsoft Word may be your best software choice.

You may be tempted to use your word processor's "mail merge" feature. This allows you to customize form letters so they look as though they're personal ones. Most job counselors caution that form letters produce poor results and employers can spot the personalized bits that mail merge programs insert. It's a good idea to focus each letter you send on the specific employer and opening. Of course, there will be paragraphs you include in every letter, but employers are looking for sincere interest in their organizations. If you don't consider yourself a good writer, increase the boilerplate paragraphs and decrease the custom-written sections, but don't start with a form letter.

Using a Multi-function Software Suite

Microsoft Works is an example of a program that has several different modules that can perform a variety of tasks. MS Works comes already installed on many new Windows-based computers. Microsoft Office is another example of what's often called a software suite. If you choose MS Word as your word-processing program, you will find it easier to use the other modules in the suite, so you can explore the Excel spreadsheet module, the Access database module, and the PowerPoint presentation module. Once you have become comfortable with one module, you will discover that the others, which use many of the same menus, look very familiar.

Check Your E-mail

You probably have an e-mail address, either at home or at work, and you use it at least occasionally. It is essential that you spend some time every day on your home computer, so get into the habit of corresponding with more friends and family members in this way. Naturally, you enjoy hearing from your children and grandchildren who may be scattered all over the country or even across the globe. It is even possible to track down childhood friends and college roommates. The more positive computer experiences you have, the more comfortable you will become. The frustration of computer crashes and other crises are balanced by the pleasure of staying in touch with friends. It is even possible to make "phone calls" using your computer's microphone and speaker. You can talk as long as you like at no additional cost.

If you begin using Microsoft Outlook on a regular basis (not Outlook Express), you may want to copy and paste important information into the Contacts section, especially the signature files that most business people insert automatically at the bottom of their e-mails. Because the Outlook program is already loaded, it's easy to copy other information into your calendar. For example, if you have an interview, you can copy not only the date and time, but also driving directions and any other information that will better prepare you.

Having Fun With a Computer

Finding enjoyable things to do with your computer will certainly improve your attitude, but you may still find yourself looking at it as some kind of mechanical monster. Learning to use a computer is not really very different from learning any other skill, but there is one big difference. You know perfectly well that a camera or a VCR is a machine that performs certain functions. Although this is true of computers as well, the popular media are constantly telling you that computers are different. They are not machines but superbrains, far more intelligent than our own.

We have all seen dozens of movies and TV shows in which computers take over the world. They function completely on their own, making decisions with no input from human beings. As Hal is in the film *2001: A Space Odyssey,* they may be evil, power-crazed monsters intent on interplanetary domination. On the other hand, they may be cute and well meaning, such as Robbie the Robot or C3-PO, nurturing and benevolent, but ever so much more intelligent than their human companions.

These mental pictures are always in the back of our minds and pop up when a computer malfunctions. When something unexpected happens, we assume that the brilliant computer mind is deliberately trying to frustrate us. We are in a battle of wits with a far more intelligent opponent and can never win. Try very hard to erase these images from your memory or at least accept the fact that they belong entirely to the world of fantasy. Computers are machines and nothing more than machines. They have all been designed, built, and programmed by human beings. They can do nothing that those human beings have not taught them. No computer even begins to approach your brain in intelligence and complexity. Computers may do what they do much more quickly—at the speed of electrons—but they totally lack your flexibility.

Getting Your Typing Up to Speed

If, many long years ago, you took a typing course in high school, you are well ahead of the game. Just a general idea where the keys are located is probably enough to get you started. Unfortunately, it used to be considered unmanly for boys to learn to type. Men were trained to become captains of industry who would be much too busy and important to do their own typing. Because typing was a "womanly" skill, girls got a big head start. Nevertheless, typing with a computer is really very easy. Many of those skills that were needed for big clunky manual typewriters are no longer important. Errors can be corrected so easily that sometimes it isn't even worth trying to avoid them. You may soon find yourself typing almost as fast as you can think because you can always go back later to fix glaring problems.

Many typing tutor software programs are available ranging from amusing ones intended for small children up to complete adult courses. "Mavis Beacon Teaches Typing" is probably the best known, but there are dozens of others. Many are inexpensive shareware programs that can be downloaded from the Internet. I personally used a children's program that required me to zap letters as they fell from the top of the screen. If I didn't manage to hit the right keys before they reached the ground (or the bottom of the screen), they exploded with a loud bang. There are much less violent programs available, but the exploding letters game had me typing more or less adequately within just a few weeks.

Do You Really Need Your Own Computer?

Let us say that you have been using a public computer lab for job-hunting activities. You may not be a whiz, but you are beginning to feel more confident. Is it time to make the plunge and invest in your own computer? Of course, your personal finances will have a lot to do with the decision, but there are other considerations as well.

Take a moment to think about the tasks related to your job search that you are able to do on a public computer. Most public computers have a word-processing program so you can write letters and type a resume. You are not, however, able to save these files on a public computer. Because you will not want to compose each letter for each job opening from scratch, you will need to find a way to save files. Perhaps the most efficient way to do this is to purchase a small flash memory drive. Priced from approximately $20, these are actually very small, very portable hard drives that you can put in your pocket or attach to your key chain. Even the small-capacity flash drives will probably be adequate for your needs. However, you will need to check with the staff member who supervises your public computer lab to see whether you are permitted to use one. Because they must be plugged into the public computer's USB port, some technicians fear that flash drives might infect their computers with a virus or spyware. In that case, you can save your files onto floppy disks or CD-ROMs if they are permitted. However, if you are unable to save your work, you will find yourself becoming frustrated.

Gradually, as you become a more active computer user, you will discover other limitations of public computers and begin considering the purchase of your own computer. When you have your own computer, no one else can download viruses or play games while you wait impatiently. No one can accidentally corrupt the word-processing program just when you want to write a letter or tell you that your time is up when your application is due tomorrow. Sharing computers with hundreds of students or library patrons often means they're unavailable when you need them or in such poor condition that your file may disappear at any moment. However, you will be on your own and you will need to solve your own problems. How independent have you become? How often do you still need help? If you are using a public computer lab, can you work alone for an hour or so without assistance? Because you're still developing your skills, it's natural that you will continue to need help with new challenges, but do you feel as if you've mastered the basics?

Laptop Computers

If you do a lot of traveling, you may be thinking that it would be nice to have a small laptop computer that you can take with you. It's true that laptops are nice to have when you're on the road, but they probably should not be chosen over a more substantial, stay-at-home desktop computer. Laptop monitors are sometimes difficult to see, even for younger people whose vision is probably better than yours. Their keyboards are also smaller. Your hands quickly feel cramped and you tend to make many more errors than on a standard keyboard. Especially irritating are the built-in gizmos that substitute for the mouse. They are hard to use, so highlighting text or clicking on a link can become a chore.

If, however, you really do need to cart a computer around with you, you might invest in what's called a "docking station." This allows you to plug in your laptop computer and add whatever other peripheral equipment you need (such as a full-sized keyboard and mouse, or a larger monitor). The laptop can then be used as a desktop computer when it's more convenient, but it can also go on the road with you once you disconnect the extra equipment.

Choosing a Computer

For many of us, the thought of purchasing a computer is quite intimidating. First, of course, it represents a substantial investment, even if you choose a used one. Advertisements for computers appear to be written in Greek and proclaim features that mean absolutely nothing to you. Salesmen use the same incomprehensible gibberish, and you're left with no more information than you started with. How, then, should you choose a computer?

Talking to friends about their computer choices can be very helpful. However, you may encounter a lot of conflicting advice. Your library probably carries a number of computer magazines. Some examples are *PC World, PC Computing,* and *Home Office Computing.* Look through some of the more popular ones, though probably not the most recent issues. The computers that are reviewed in the current issue are state-of-the-art, selling at peak prices. You will probably want to wait until the prices have come down to affordable levels.

As you read reviews and talk to friends and technicians, be sure to ask about service. As a new computer owner, you're going to need help. If you are able to phone a technician and explain your difficulty, he or she may be able to solve it in minutes. If, on the other hand, you get a recorded message and your call is not returned for days, a small problem can easily turn into a major crisis. Look for service contracts that include a phone number that you can call free of charge. Make note of whether a repair person will come to your home or you will have to bring your computer to a service center for repair. A warranty on parts is also important. Many computer users, however, will tell you that they are happier purchasing only minimal technical support with their new computer and then hiring a local person who is willing to make house calls.

Choosing Software Programs

When you're learning to use a computer program, you need friends. If you're struggling with a manual that sounds as if it were written in a foreign language, there's nothing as wonderful as a friend or computer lab technician who knows the program. He or she can get you over a hurdle that's caused you hours of misery with a just a few well-chosen words. For this reason, you might choose a program that's popular among your friends even if it costs a little more.

Avoiding Crises

Novice computer users are often discouraged by the horror stories they hear from friends and coworkers. Crises do indeed happen, so it's important to be prepared. When you save a file, you're depending on magnetic impulses that grow faint over time. Computer hard drives and other storage media have very limited life expectancies. CD-ROM disks are easily scratched, making data impossible to read. Be sure that, in an emergency, you have backup file copies. Consider what you would do if your computer's hard drive "died" or if your resume file suddenly disappeared. It often seems that just having the plan assures that you'll never have to use it.

The stereotype of the computer-challenged boomer is so prevalent that many employers will make that assumption about you unless you prove to them that you are different. This is not a battle that can be won with words. You will need to exude a computer comfort level that is similar to younger staff members. Remember that they spend many hours a day with a computer, both at home and on the job. To achieve a similar comfort level, you are going to need to find ways to integrate the computer into most of your daily activities. This is a lot different than checking your e-mail once in a while. Real computer literacy represents a huge commitment, but you will find it well worth the effort.

Going Back to the Classroom

David spent more than 25 years working as a civil servant. He gradually climbed the career ladder of local government administration and achieved a measure of status and financial comfort. It happened that the city that employed David had a reputation for corruption, but David's own department stayed reasonably free of political influence. Most of his colleagues worked hard and took their work seriously. This was not true of some other departments, however, and the mayor's office was widely known as "corruption central."

Nevertheless, the mayor was getting old and, when a reform movement swept the city, he could no longer hold back the tide of change. He was succeeded by a reform administration full of "young Turks" who were determined to root out corruption at every level. Unfortunately, when the new broom swept clean, it made no distinction between the good guys and the bad guys.

Newly hired young people were brought in to straighten out every department, and David was suddenly a symbol of the bad old days. Because it was nearly impossible to fire a longtime worker, especially one who had earned nothing short of glowing evaluations, the "young Turks" set David to work doing mindless tasks and tried to pretend he wasn't there. These constant wounds to his ego turned work into torture. David, however, was only in his early 50s and he needed to maximize his retirement benefits. One affront to his dignity followed another until David knew that, even if he spent the rest of his life in poverty, he had to leave. But what was he going to do with his life? Thoroughly demoralized, he wondered what, if anything, he might possibly be good at.

Rekindling the Dream

Looking back at his college years, David remembered how much he had wanted to become an English professor. However, his practical side won the day. Earning both a master's degree and a Ph.D. in English, when employment prospects were limited, was not a reasonable goal. Instead, he chose a career in government that provided safety, opportunity for advancement, and excellent benefits. For 25 years, it seemed he had made the right choice.

One evening after an especially agonizing day at work, David decided he had to make a decision; he couldn't go on this way! First he gathered up all the paperwork he had filed away on his pension plan and investments. Then he sat down at his kitchen table and figured out exactly how much money he would have available if he were to resign immediately. It wasn't much, that was for sure, but he wouldn't starve. However, there was a big difference between merely existing and enjoying a satisfying and meaningful life. What would he do with his time? Seemingly out of nowhere, that old ambition popped into his head. But that was ridiculous, he argued with himself. He couldn't become a college professor now. The cost of a Ph.D. would be astronomical, and by the time he completed the degree he'd have just a few years left to pursue a career.

Making Plans

That night David couldn't sleep. His practical self kept trying to regain control, but by 4 a.m., it was clear that the idealistic dreamer had won. At 8:30, he called in sick. In the 25 years he had worked for the city, David had never claimed illness just to get a day off, but this day was different. The next thing he did was to make an appointment with an admissions counselor at a local state university and another appointment with the chair of the English department. David expected to feel as comfortable as a fish out of water on the university campus. He dreaded explaining his problems to a counselor and an English professor who were both younger than he. In a nutshell, he hated admitting he was a failure.

Older Students Are Welcome

The two meetings, however, turned out to be very different from what he expected. In general, universities welcome older students. They know so much more about themselves and their abilities than young people fresh out of high school. Although David had imagined that he would be the oldest graduate student in the university, it turned out that there were hundreds of other students in his age bracket. Some were earning degrees to become eligible for promotion. Others, like David, were preparing for entirely new careers. Neither of the people David met seemed surprised or shocked at his impractical goal. In fact, it turned out it was not so impractical after all. The cost of in-state tuition was relatively low, and teaching assistantships and other part-time jobs kept most graduate students from dire poverty.

How Large a Commitment?

It was true, however, that earning two graduate degrees would take a lot of time. It would mean spending several years attending classes, conducting research, writing papers, and studying for examinations. As we get older, our time becomes more important to us. Did David really want to devote so much time to education? He remembered, however, all those courses he had been taking just for fun. By this point, he had nearly exhausted the offerings of his local community college, but he remembered how good the mental stimulation from those history, writing, and computer courses felt.

A few days later, he sat down at the kitchen table once again. By this time, however, there were so many papers piled on it that he had begun eating in the living room. After all those years as a civil servant, David was good at paper-work, and he certainly needed that skill now. The university's application form was several pages long, and he would have to send for transcripts of all his academic work since high school. The equally complicated scholarship applications and financial aid forms would also take a lot of work. Just now, however, David had to decide how he would pay his bills.

The Unexpected Benefits of Being a Student

Perhaps his biggest worry was already solved. Part of the reason he had waited so long to resign was that he needed health insurance. His policy with the city paid for most of his expenses and, at his age, he dared not take chances. Many boomers hold on to their boring and unpleasant jobs for this reason alone. Although he could extend his coverage with COBRA for 18 months, it would be expensive, and he would have no health insurance after COBRA expired. As a university student, however, he would be entitled to participate in an excellent healthcare plan and his costs would be lower than COBRA. Healthcare insurers can offer low rates because most college and university students are young and have few medical expenses. That means that, by participating in the group, David could enjoy considerable savings.

Establishing a Budget

The discovery that he would be eligible for an inexpensive healthcare plan set David to recalculating the long row of numbers he had been jotting down. If he tapped his pension and retirement account benefits now, he would reduce his income later when he might not be able to work. On the other hand, if he cut out some luxuries that didn't mean a lot to him, he could probably get by without touching his retirement income. His savings would cover emergencies, and, if it turned out he had underestimated his financial needs, he was young enough to reevaluate his options.

David is now writing his doctoral dissertation. He has earned a master's degree and passed the comprehensive examinations required to begin work on his dissertation. He is looking forward to the time when he can apply for a full-time teaching position and begin enjoying some of those luxuries beyond the reach of most graduate students. Nevertheless, he knows that he made the right decision.

Some Things Get Easier, Some Get Harder

Some things have turned out to be harder than he expected. For example, taking the required Graduate Record Exam gets more difficult as you get older. Even though your general knowledge increases, your short-term memory begins declining in your 40s. Older students are also more plagued with test anxiety and may not do well on timed tests. Fortunately, universities are accustomed to working with older students and can ease or minimize some of these problems.

David, however, excelled in his coursework. Unlike when he was in college, he could take classes he really enjoyed. Instructors, whose days are packed with bored 19-year-olds insisting they deserve higher test grades, enjoy having mature adults in their classes. Just as long as these older students are open to new ideas and don't insist on monopolizing the class, their presence is sought after and appreciated. After two years of feeling inept and unwanted at work, David basked in the warm glow of academic success.

The Rewards of Learning

Most of us realize that if we're going to start a new career or begin a job that requires new skills, we may need to go back to school. However, more and more boomers are finding that, whatever their plans, getting back into the classroom is a good choice. Not only will it improve their chances of on-the-job success, but it will enhance their quality of life in unexpected ways. Many say that it isn't so much what they learn; it is the fact that they are learning. The classroom environment gives them a chance not only to update their skills but also to become more comfortable with today's world.

Even before you're ready to launch into a job hunt, it's a good idea to sign up for a course at your local community college. Many boomers choose to take a computer class, but it doesn't really matter what you choose. In fact, it might be a good idea to choose your first class mostly for fun. Choose a hobby you enjoy and would like to learn more about. Maybe you're an avid gardener or enjoy repairing your own car. One of the best things about taking such a course is that your classmates are similar to you: They're really interested in the subject. Sharing this interest will bring you into contact with people of all ages and backgrounds.

As we get older, our worlds tend to narrow. We gradually limit our experiences, talking with the same people, watching the same television programs, and following the same routines. Most boomers find that they now enjoy learning just for its own sake. They report that charging up their mental batteries feels good, lifts their spirits, and even energizes them. Later, when you know the direction you want to take, whether it's changing jobs or starting a business, you'll be better prepared for the classroom. If you hit some stumbling blocks, you will be able to deal with them before getting serious about formal study.

Your Brain's Just Fine

Stumbling blocks? What stumbling blocks? Your antennae may be tingling because, deep down, you're afraid that maybe you've lost your academic skills. In reality, you'll probably find that if you were once a good student, you'll still be a good student; if you disliked school as a child, you may find it much more enjoyable now that you have experience and maturity under your belt. I think it's fair to say that the pluses and minuses of getting older almost cancel one another out in the classroom, but the pluses have a slight edge.

As we mentioned, your short-term memory is probably not what it was when you were 19. You may once have stayed up late the night before a test and crammed huge amounts of information into your brain. The next day you transferred all those facts to your test paper. For most boomers, this no longer works. Your brain simply will not behave as a sponge anymore. Isolated facts are unlikely to register.

However, you have something that may be even more useful than that undiscriminating, undiscerning sponge: You have led a life filled with experiences, and those experiences stay with you, forming an organized network of ideas and information. New facts and ideas can each find a place in that network. They are integrated with other ideas and become far more meaningful than isolated facts. Nevertheless, everything will take more time. You'll need more time to study for a test and more time to answer the test questions. A research paper that another student might do in a few days will take you a week or more.

When Egos Clash

Not everyone who goes back to the classroom is as successful as David. Stan is an example of a boomer who just couldn't put aside his inflated ego. He, too, enrolled in a program at his local university. Because he'd always had a gift for languages, Stan decided to pursue a degree in Japanese. Stan had always been fascinated by Japanese culture, and he'd become proficient in several languages since college, so he expected to have no problems with the subject.

Stan was perfectly correct that he could handle the subject matter. His brain had been active over the years, and all those neurons needed little retraining to master Japanese. The problem was that Stan saw himself as special, or at least he wanted to see himself that way. Younger people were "full of themselves" and just didn't appreciate his superior abilities. Unfortunately, he did not keep these thoughts to himself. When fellow students made friendly overtures, he seized the opportunity to tell them about himself—all about himself—every accomplishment and every brilliant idea he'd ever had. You can easily imagine their reaction. Students sitting at nearby study desks moved away during the break and made a point of avoiding his eyes after class.

Stan also liked to answer the instructor's questions. He made a point of always being prepared for class and wanted to make sure everyone knew how smart he was. Young people are much more reticent about speaking in class. They hold back and generally frown on what they call "brownnosing" the professor. Young people are seldom taking a course for the fun of it, and they view older students such as Stan as showoffs.

At first Stan's instructors appreciated his enthusiasm. It is depressing to be continually asking questions that are met with dead silence, and it is nice to know that at least one student is interested in the class. Soon, however, they grew tired of his long-winded monologues. Stan's comments took up far too much time and kept the class from learning more important information. To make matters worse, Stan often thought he knew more than the instructor. Sometimes he was right and sometimes he was wrong, but in the end he made himself *persona non grata* to faculty members. To be effective, college instructors must maintain the respect and attention of their classes. They naturally resent being made to look foolish and they fear losing control. Stan was so focused on himself and his own contributions that he never saw his teachers as people who needed his loyalty and support.

Becoming a Student Again

In general, it is a good idea to imitate the behavior of the other students. By this I don't mean descending to the level of bored and unresponsive 19-year-olds who make it clear that they would rather be doing almost anything else. Instead, keep a low profile until you see how the better students interact with the instructor and with one another. Appear interested in the class but don't monopolize discussions. You might even count the number of times you speak and put yourself on a strict allowance.

Remember that younger instructors may feel intimidated by your presence. Make it a point to tell them how much you enjoy the class and don't bring every small mistake to their attention. There is no need to impress them with your knowledge. They are, in a sense, giving you the fruits of their research and study. Accept it as a gift, and don't look the gift horse in the mouth.

Get to know your classmates, but let them do most of the talking. One of the most positive aspects of going back to school is getting to know younger people as peers. You are all equals and you are all sharing a common experience. Take advantage of that bond to get to know them better. Seeing the world through their eyes will prepare you for the job market, as it is younger people who dominate it.

Full- or Part-Time?

Going back to the classroom can mean anything from a single course to a multi-year commitment, as in David's case. It can mean just a little mental exercise, or it can be the beginning a whole new lifestyle. It is probably a good idea to get your feet wet before you make a major commitment. You may remember that David had been taking courses at his local community college. He first took computer courses when he began to feel that he was not keeping up with younger people in his government office. However, each semester when he checked the list of classes, he found other courses that sounded interesting. Gradually, especially when the courses he wanted were not being offered, he delved deeper and experimented with subjects he knew absolutely nothing about. In some cases, he concluded that he had been wise to avoid them but in others, he discovered new interests and aptitudes.

When David resigned from his full-time job, he had both a new career objective and eight hours each day that was no longer occupied. Because he had a clear goal and wanted to prepare himself for a position as an English professor as quickly as possible, he enrolled as a full-time student. Stan, on the other hand, had always been interested in languages.

A new language under his belt served as a kind of "open sesame!" to a different and fascinating culture. Traveling to far off places is much more interesting when you can actually talk with the local people without a translator. You are able to make new friends and see firsthand how they really live. It is possible to pursue this kind of goal by becoming a part-time student.

Some boomers begin as part-time students so that they will have plenty of time and energy to devote to their classes. As they become more confident of their ability, they gradually increase their course load. It is important that your first forays into the academic world are both enjoyable and successful. Be careful not to allow yourself to become overtired or overwhelmed with work. If you take on too much when you're starting out, you may become discouraged and imagine that you are not cut out for the classroom—a conclusion that may be far from true.

When Does Your Brain Wake Up?

Back in the old days when you were a high school or college student, you had a lot more energy than you do now, but there were times when you were not at your best. For example, you knew you were not a morning person and avoided 8 a.m. classes, or maybe you snoozed in the afternoon when the course was less than exciting. Now that you're older, you have lost some of that youthful liveliness and those "downtimes" have increased.

It's important to take your energy level into consideration and schedule both your classes and your study periods at times when your brain is working. Many of us find it difficult to go to class after a full day at the office. If you find yourself tempted to curl up on the sofa after work, why not take a course during your lunch hour and work a little later that day? Experiment with different schedules to get the most out of your classroom experience—but be sure your boss approves of any changes to your work schedule. The last thing you need when you're job-hunting is a poor reference. Keep in mind, too, that some colleges and universities offer weekend classes. They provide complete saturation in a subject from Friday until Sunday. For some people, this is the perfect way to learn a subject; for others it is utterly exhausting.

You Need a Support System

Most colleges and universities have academic assistance or support centers that are not fully used. Only at exam time are they crowded with students who have suddenly realized they're in trouble. If you are unsure about your ability to take college courses, it's a good idea to set up a regular appointment with a counselor or tutor. Become familiar with the tutoring and other support programs available and find out which staff members best understand the needs of older students. In general, older counselors understand older students, but this isn't always the case. There are always going to be some people with whom you can communicate more easily than others. You might begin by dropping in at a convenient time and meeting with whoever is available. Once you discover someone who understands your needs, set up a regular appointment with him or her.

Many older students like to have a tutor go over their written reports and research papers. They find that, because they have not written anything but business letters for the past 30 years, they may be careless about grammar or have trouble putting words together. If you think you fit into this category, you might want to take a writing or composition course while you are still working at your old job.

Staying Fit

Most colleges and universities offer their students exercise and fitness facilities. Top-of-the-line exercise equipment such as treadmills, exercise bikes, and stair steppers are free (or available at nominal cost) to students. Many campus fitness centers even have indoor, Olympic-sized swimming pools. While you're busy changing your lifestyle, don't forget that good health is one of your most important goals. Don't waste this wonderful opportunity to stay fit. Other people pay hefty fees to belong to fitness clubs and spas, whereas you have access to an outstanding facility just a few steps from your classroom. You can enjoy a quick workout or splash in the pool anytime you're on campus.

Treasure Your Student ID

Although there are many more important reasons to go back to the classroom, don't forget that you become entitled to a wide variety of student perks. Your student ID entitles you to special rates and discounts on many of the goods and services you need. Especially attractive are treasures that await you at your campus bookstore. Did you know that most software companies produce educational versions of their software programs that are nearly identical to the high-priced business versions? Take, for example, the Microsoft Office suite. The list price for the professional edition is about $500; the educational version, which includes most of the same bells and whistles, is available to bona fide students for less than $200. Many universities negotiate with software producers for even better prices and may even offer some programs (anti-virus software, for example) to their students free of charge.

Summing It Up

Going back to the classroom, however, is not about getting better deals on software, plane tickets, or movie matinees. It's really about you and how you feel about yourself. As a boomer, you can expect to live many years after your 60th birthday, and you want them to be the best years of your life. Happy people are growing and changing with every year they live. They don't sit back and watch the world pass them by. Think back on people you know from your parents' generation. Some of them were old at 60, whereas others stayed interested in life, planning new adventures and investigating new ideas. Going back to school is not the only way to stay connected to life, but many boomers will tell you it made all the difference to them.

Triumphing at the Interview

During your career, you have probably been invited to a dozen or more job interviews. You may have carefully prepared before each one and even followed the tips given in the many "how-to" books on the subject. Much of this experience and advice is still useful to you, but there are some new hurdles that boomers must contend with.

In Chapter 8, you spiffed up your on-the-job image, giving yourself a contemporary look that is more in step with younger people in the business world. You took an honest look at yourself, became more careful about your diet, established an exercise regimen, and generally set to work on improving your health and your physical appearance. Although you may look your age, an interviewer's first impression should be of a healthy, well-dressed, enthusiastic boomer who could fit comfortably into an organization.

What to Expect

In the typical job interview, an experienced manager interviews a younger, less-experienced applicant. Now the tables are turned. You, the seasoned veteran, will be interviewed by a younger man or woman who may have only a fraction of your experience. In the past, you were encouraged to try to impress the interviewer with your skills and experience. Of course, it's still important to appear competent. However, if you overdo it, you may end up monopolizing the interview and boring the interviewer with a lengthy monologue. In the how-to books, you are advised to redirect the interview, when necessary, to emphasize your qualifications. However,

179

the older you get, the more experience you acquire—much of which has no connection to the job you've applied for. In your anxiety to appear as the best-qualified applicant, you may, instead, come across as a know-it-all who talks too much and who will insist on doing things your own way.

Honing Your Answers

Just as it is necessary to sculpt your resume into a slimmer, more manageable form, so too you will want to sculpt your responses at the interview. Which of your skills, courses, and work experiences are directly relevant to this job? Which can be made to sound as if they might be steps on a career ladder that leads to this particular position? Choose just a few. You have an advantage over younger applicants in that you can pick and choose from a long career. Carefully pick out the points you want to get across. If you don't know exactly what the job involves, you might want to hold an experience or two in reserve, but don't give in to the temptation to show off during the interview. Don't launch on a list of past experiences, and be sure that you respond directly to the questions asked. It is true that you may need to include some information without being asked, but keep these contributions to a minimum. If you bore your interviewer, you will certainly not be remembered as the best candidate.

Projecting Confidence

Possibly the best way to go into an interview is with the firm conviction that you are far and away the best-qualified, absolutely perfect applicant for the position. By some strange coincidence, this is also the ideal job for you. If you can really project conviction without appearing over-confident, you can probably get the job. Remember that you are not too good for the job; you are just right. You are neither overqualified nor under-qualified. Like the porridge in the story of the three bears, this job is just right. It is a wonderful opportunity that you will be delighted to accept. Both you and the employer are lucky to have found one another, and great things will come out of the relationship.

Of course, you don't want to say this in so many words. It should be implicit in your attitude, your enthusiasm, and your relaxed self-confidence. It should be tempered, however, with just a little caution.

Avoiding Overconfidence

Whereas quiet confidence will score points, talky, opinionated overconfidence should be avoided. I recently met a woman who has an impressive background in social services but lost her job in a recent cutback. Although she has received state and regional awards for her work, she is finding that she simply cannot get another job. A forceful, assured woman, she exudes confidence when she goes into a job interview. To prove to me that she was the victim of discrimination, she gave me a play-by-play account of her most recent interview.

Although I was not a fly on the wall during the actual interview, I cannot imagine how the interviewer said more than a few words. Once the woman got started, she simply took over. If you were the interviewer, it is doubtful that you would be positively impressed. You would wonder how on earth you could train this person to be a productive employee. If she felt compelled to do all the talking, how could she really become part of a team? As a boss, you might value independence and initiative, but essentially you need a staff member who will do the job within the limits you set. This applicant would surely remake the job to her own specifications.

Sometimes, of course, you don't really believe either that the job is right for you, or that you are the best applicant. After several unsuccessful interviews, your confidence may be ebbing and self-doubt may be clouding your sunny interview personality. In that case, it will be necessary to call on your skills as an actor, stifling your doubts and insecurities for an hour or two. In other words, fake it. However, if you cannot work up some enthusiasm, maybe this isn't the right job for you.

Establishing Rapport With the Interviewer

Many successful applicants have developed what might be called a corollary to this strategy. Not only is this the perfect job but, by yet another amazing coincidence, applicant and interviewer are remarkably compatible. The rapport is instant and they can't imagine anyone they'd like to talk with more. At the core of this strategy is the notion that everyone likes to be liked. By subtly making it clear to the interviewer that you are delighted to find such an intelligent and congenial person conducting the interview, you move several notches toward the prize. In truth, you may not find the interviewer delightful company and, in your anxiety, you will probably not be thinking about camaraderie or friendship. Keep in mind, however, that the more pleasant you make the experience for the interviewer, the more enthusiastically he or she is likely to look on your application.

Not many people enjoy the job of interviewing applicants. They know that there can be only one who gets the job, and so the others will be disappointed. Most of us feel guilty at having to disappoint the majority of the people we interview. With this in mind, be careful not to quiz the interviewer about your chances of getting the job. Don't word your responses in terms of "you should give me this job because…." Although that's precisely what you will be trying to get across, rephrase your questions and comments to be more objective and less personal. Don't beg and don't tell the interviewer what he or she should do.

Because it is important that the interviewer enjoy the interview, smile frequently. Add a little humor when it's appropriate, and it's often a good idea to poke fun at yourself. An interview must include a certain amount of what, in any other circumstances, would be bragging, and humor can make it clear that you don't have a swelled head or an over-inflated view of your abilities. If you can look back on an interview and recall moments when you and the interviewer were laughing comfortably together, it's a good indicator of success. Making fun of the interviewer or the organization is usually dangerous because you're an outsider. You don't know the lay of the land, so it's easy to accidentally stumble on a sensitive issue. Making fun of political figures or current controversies can also be dangerous. It's almost always safe to use self-deprecating humor, as long as you don't appear to be pulling yourself down. Make it clear that you're comfortable in your own skin but you don't take yourself too seriously.

Focusing on Recent Experience

Although you should never deliberately misrepresent yourself, it is important to appear as similar to a younger applicant as possible, and this means emphasizing roughly the same amount of experience. Think back to a moment when you were sitting in the interviewer's chair. If an applicant described a long laundry list of different jobs, you were not positively impressed. Instead, you probably suspected that this was someone who jumped from job to job, either voluntarily or because asked to leave. In your own case, you've acquired these varied experiences not because you've job-hopped, but because you've had a long career. Nevertheless, the interviewer may not take this into consideration.

As you decide which jobs to emphasize, strip out clues that place them in another era. Don't reminisce about mainframe computers or other equipment that is no longer in use. Terminology changes over the years as well, so be careful how you describe processes and procedures. The skills you describe must sound the same as the ones you would need if you started work tomorrow, not history lessons.

Knowing When to Talk and When to Listen

Have you noticed that as you've gotten older, you talk more? Many of us have gotten wordier with the passing of time. We have more stories to tell and we enjoy telling them. This is another of the ways we differ from younger applicants who have less to say. They may be more nervous during an interview and may be awed by the interviewer. In fact, they may do little more than answer the questions asked of them.

Although you still need to subtly direct the interview, making sure you have the opportunity to present yourself as the right person for the job, an older applicant can easily overwhelm a younger boss. If you openly take control, you may end up making the interviewer feel uncomfortable. A long monologue covering all your past experience is boring and probably irrelevant. Your goal is not to tell the interviewer how wonderful you are, but how well you will fit into the organization. The young boss must be able to picture you as a subordinate who accepts direction and will be a good team member.

Thinking Young

Not only is it important to minimize differences between you and younger applicants, but it's also a good idea to find ways in which you and the interviewer are alike. Once again, remember that people naturally hire other people who are similar to them. They first imagine themselves performing the job and then look for someone who fits into their mental picture. Your job will be to minimize the differences and emphasize the ways in which you are like the interviewer. This, of course, means de-emphasizing the age difference, but you also want to make it clear that you both approach a job the same way—that you share the same values, priorities, and interests.

Controlling Nervous Chatter

This reminds me of a friend who has always had a hard time with job interviews. Once hired, he usually does well and receives frequent promotions. However, getting his foot in the door is always a challenge. The reason is not hard to discover. Even when young, he talked too much. A stressful situation seemed to turn on an unstoppable flow of words.

I was never at one of his interviews, so I can't be certain, but I can imagine him coming across as an annoying soap salesman. Even before telemarketers, pushy salesmen had a bad reputation. Our defenses go up immediately when we fear we are being pressured into doing something we don't really want to do. Instead of doing all the talking yourself, find ways to encourage the interviewer to talk. Before the interview, reread whatever information you have available about the job and the organization. Think of several appropriate questions, and have them ready for moments when the interviewer's enthusiasm seems to be waning. Revive the interview not with your own comments but with your questions.

Winning Friends and Influencing People

Although excessive reticence in an interview is not desirable, interviewers may actually prefer an applicant who lets them do most of the talking. It has long been known, even before Dale Carnegie made it a household expression, that the best way to "win friends and influence people" is to let them talk. Once again, think back to a time when you were in the interviewer's chair. You were probably impressed by the applicants who shared your vision of the job. If it were possible to replay a tape of those interviews, you might discover that, although they did a competent job of answering your questions, what put them over the top were their enthusiastic expressions of interest and frequent nods of agreement.

Likewise, remember that you have developed strong opinions over the years. Decide which of them are safe to express in an interview and which might possibly give rise to a negative reaction. Because we enjoy talking, especially talking about ourselves, we may unconsciously look on the interview as an opportunity to discuss our opinions on politics, current events, and even religion. A few years ago I was the interviewer, talking with an older job applicant. I had the impression the poor man was starved for someone to listen to him. It was impossible to keep the interview on track, and I was eventually forced to end it abruptly. By the time I was able to make it clear that I had other things to do, I had heard his opinions on every hot-button issue since World War II, including a long harangue on the sad state of the modern world.

Let me caution you against any discussion of the good old days. Younger applicants were not around during those good old days, so you are immediately pointing out your differences. The interviewer very likely wasn't around then either, so you are pegged as an "old codger." Whenever possible, focus on the present and the future, and be sure that future is a bright and sunny one. If you think the world is going to the dogs, keep it to yourself.

Remembering to Be Humble

Earlier in the book I described unhappy boomers who used to be important. As you'll remember, these are people who held somewhat impressive positions in the past. They continue to measure success by their former place in the corporate pecking order. Please, please don't tell the interviewer that you used to be important. You've made a decision to get out of the rat race and find a job that really uses your talents and truly meets your needs. It's difficult for young interviewers to understand this. They are still back there trying to establish their own place in the pecking order. Therefore, if you insist on talking about all the important jobs you had, you'll be seen as a failure. You'll be picturing yourself as a "has been" when that is exactly what you are not.

You are beginning a new and highly rewarding part of your life. You need not try to convince interviewers that you were important because they are not looking for an important job. Your past can be useful to you now because it allowed you to develop skills and gain experience that prepared you for this new phase of your life. Emphasize those skills and not the positions themselves. In general, you can assume that most supervisors do not want to hire subordinates who once held higher-level positions than their own. With some justification, they tend to believe that such employees would be hard to supervise. What they do want are employees who will learn the job quickly, so relevant past experience is helpful. Thus your past experience can work for you or it can work against you.

The Pre-interview Phone Call

Although employers often schedule telephone interviews, they (not their assistants) may also call you without warning. The reasons they give may be to clarify your qualifications or find out when you might be free for an interview. In fact, they might give any of a number of reasons for calling, but their real reason is to get a quick sense of who you are. These employers, usually mistakenly, imagine that if they can just talk with you for a few minutes, they will know instinctively whether you're worth an interview. Possibly, your application package just arrived on their desk; their eye rests on your phone number. What could be more natural than picking up the phone?

When You're on the Spot

From your point of view, you'd rather not be put on the spot this way, but you have no choice in the matter. You're going to need a plan to deal with the unexpected call, and the first part of the plan calls for a change in the way you answer your phone. While you're in job-hunting mode, make sure your answering machine or voice-mail message communicates the right image. Work out an understanding with the other members of your household that yours will be the voice that callers hear, and that voice will be pleasant and professional. You won't tell jokes or play music, and you'll record the message only when you can eliminate background noise. If you put more than one phone number on your resume, be sure that callers will get the same message no matter which number they dial. If you don't subscribe to caller ID, it might be a good idea to do so. That way, you will be aware of callers who don't leave messages.

Once you have taken care of the calls you missed, what about the ones that reach you? You might start by examining the way you usually answer the phone. In the last few years, many people have begun answering their phones in a voice that is clearly suspicious, as if they are expecting a telemarketer or other unwanted intrusion. Such a voice is not the one you want a potential employer to hear. For the duration of your job hunt, answer each phone call in a warm, well-modulated tone of voice. You'll brighten the day of weary telemarketers, but you'll also communicate a positive image of yourself to employers. Those first words can make all the difference.

Expecting the Unexpected

What do you say after you say, "Hello"? Again, you want to keep your voice pleasant and well modulated. Appear familiar with the callers' names, even if you've sent out a dozen applications and you're hazy about the recipients. Appear happy that they called, even if it is a somewhat inconvenient time. If you can't talk (if for instance you're called at work), your challenge will be to let callers know how much you'd enjoy talking with them, but you will have to call them back later. Try to find a mutually agreeable time when you both will be free and make an effort to be the one who initiates the call. Occasionally, the caller will say that it's not important enough to call back. In this case, you're probably going to have to throw caution to the winds and take advantage of the one opportunity you may ever have to make a positive impression. This brings up the subject of cell phones and landlines. In general, cell phones are not reliable enough for telephone interviews. The line drops just as you are about to make your most important point. However, employers tend to call during normal business hours, and that's when you're likely to be at work. If you are dependent on your desk phone, there may be no way to converse without an audience. If, however, you have a cell phone, you can step outside and continue the conversation. If questioned later, you can explain that you had to leave the office because of a poor connection.

Be Prepared

Let's assume, however, that you are free to talk. Because you have so much invested in this phone call, you want to leave as little as possible to chance. You're going to need some kind of "cheat sheet" close to the telephone. Of course, it's difficult to read and talk at the same time, so this should be a very brief list of the jobs you've applied for, the organizations, and the individuals to whom your application packages were addressed. If you were able to do some research, summarize it very briefly in outline form. Your eye should be able to scan it quickly without losing track of the telephone conversation. You might keep your "cheat sheet" in a loose-leaf binder right under the telephone. Be sure to include a pen and some blank paper, because you will want to take notes on the call.

Now sit down! If possible, answer the phone at your desk so you can sit in a comfortable chair and have a good solid surface to write on. Don't pace around the house carrying a cordless phone. In fact, you may want to make sure that the phone you pick up is an old-fashioned one with a cord attached to the receiver. Avoid answering a cell phone when you are driving. You will need to give your full attention to the call. If you don't want to chance losing the opportunity, pull over to the side of the road or into a parking lot.

Because you're unprepared, it will be easier if the caller does most of the talking. Write out several general questions, and keep them readily available in your loose-leaf binder. Respond with plenty of enthusiasm and make it clear that your experience dovetails perfectly (or almost perfectly) with his or her needs. Remember, however, that the reason for the call is to determine whether you are "okay"—and "okay," to a large extent, means likeable. You're the kind of person the caller enjoys talking to. Warmth and enthusiasm are the qualities you must communicate no matter what direction the conversation takes.

The Pre-interview Once-Over

If you pick up or submit application materials in person, you may also have an unexpected opportunity to meet the employer. Many an unwitting job applicant, casually dressed in jeans and t-shirt, has stopped by to pick up an application on the way to the grocery store. What to his wondering eyes should appear but the manager or other decision-maker who will be evaluating applications. Even though you will usually encounter no one more formidable than the receptionist, don't take chances. You don't have to don your best interview suit, but make sure you're presentably dressed and can shake hands without worrying about your dirty fingernails.

Surviving the Telephone Interview

The current emphasis on teams in the workplace has given birth to a kind of interview that is considered by some to be the most difficult. Let's say that you have applied for a position that was advertised in the newspaper. A team or committee has been given the responsibility of choosing a group of finalists who will ultimately be considered for the position. Since the job was advertised, they have received a large number of applications and, to save time, have decided to telephone the applicants who appear to have the best qualifications. This is not unusual; in fact, many managers do the same thing. However, there's all the difference in the world between a conversation with one person and an interview with four or five people all clustered around a speakerphone.

The Tale of One Telephone Interview

To better explain what I mean, imagine that last week you received a phone call from a secretary, who explained that the hiring committee would like to talk with you. She asked if you'd be available for a conference call at a certain time. The term *conference call* is misleading. In a real conference call, each participant is connected separately from his or her office. Whether because it's easier or cheaper, committees often choose to simply gather in a room with a telephone. Once the call has been connected, the "speaker" button is pressed and, suddenly, you are talking to the whole group. Although this seems simple enough, it can easily turn into chaos. The following is a not-quite-typical scenario.

You have made arrangements to be at home and you are sitting by the phone at the appointed hour. Yet nothing happens. (That's because the committee is taking care of some preliminary business or no one can remember how the speakerphone works.) Your anxiety level rises until finally the phone rings, causing you to leap out of your seat, tangle your feet in the phone cord, and send the telephone clattering to the floor.

Retrieving the receiver and trying desperately to control your voice, you assure the group at the other end of the line that you are indeed you. The chairperson then begins reading a prepared introductory statement. You are her fourth interview this morning, so her voice is beginning to resemble the telephone recording that tells you, "That number is not in service." Next, the members of the committee introduce themselves. You hear the first one although there's a lot of static on the line; the second is a little garbled, and the third, fourth, and fifth voices are totally unintelligible. You ask them to repeat but, when you still can't hear, you decide that continued requests will make you sound like your deaf grandmother.

Someone makes a joke (you know it's a joke because the laughter comes across loud and clear). Though you have no idea what was said, you feel obligated to laugh, too. Eventually, you abandon any hope of knowing who these people are or what they do, because the chair is already reading the first prepared question. You begin your reply with enthusiasm. After a few words, you're interrupted and asked to speak a little louder. You start again, enunciating very clearly and speaking loudly into the receiver. Again, your brilliant response is interrupted while someone on the committee attempts to increase the volume on the speakerphone.

Most telephone interviews are not quite as bad as this one. Some, for instance, are real conference calls and, apart from five people repeating "Nancy (or Henry or Elizabeth), are you there?" and "Can you hear me okay?" the interview proceeds in a more or less normal fashion. From the employer's perspective, the telephone interview is a very useful innovation. Hiring committees can gather a lot of information with a minimum of effort. Resumes can be misleading, and it is quite likely that, if they depend entirely on on-site interviews and narrow the field to three or four applicants, none of those interviewed will be a good match for the job. Telephone interviews allow committees to gather additional information about 10, 15, or even more applicants. They also make efficient use of committee members' time, because several applicants can be scheduled for a single session.

These factors probably mean that the telephone interview is here to stay, so savvy boomers must find ways of surviving them. Survival means remaining in competition for the "final four" or however many applicants are selected for the in-person, on-site round. How is it possible to present a glowingly positive image under such adverse conditions? How can you establish rapport with each member of the selection committee when you can't hear what some of them are saying, can't make eye contact, and can't respond to other cues such as gestures and facial expressions? How can you keep the group awake when you're their seventh phone call, and all the applicants are beginning to sound alike? How can you avoid carrying on a personal conversation with the one person you can hear clearly, while ignoring the rest?

Preparing for the Telephone Interview

The key to success is invariably the way you prepare for the interview. Bear in mind that all the other applicants share the same playing field and experience the same handicaps. Take comfort in the fact that telephone interviews are really more predictable than their on-site counterparts, which may have a much bigger serendipity component. You can do a more effective job of anticipating questions and problems, preparing for each in turn.

Scoping Out the Territory Guerilla-Style

Let's begin with that first call, usually from a secretary or committee member, who is setting up the interview. Because this call usually comes out of the blue, you will probably be flustered or nonplused. In short, you will feel all those emotions that make it difficult to think logically and respond intelligently. Nevertheless, this is perhaps your best opportunity to gather information about the position and the people who will be interviewing you. If you don't feel quite up to absorbing this information now, ask if you may call later when you have formulated your questions.

Request the names and job titles of each of the people on the committee. In addition, discuss the job opening in as much detail as your caller feels comfortable with. If you're talking with a committee member, use the opportunity to get across a little about yourself, but don't overdo it. He or she may feel that this is more appropriate for the group. However, he or she will usually be willing to answer your questions as long as they are legitimate and don't have an "inside dope" feel about them. Ask if you might have a job description faxed to you if you don't already have one. You will also want to know how much time the committee has allotted for the telephone interview. Another applicant may be scheduled in half an hour. In that case, you will have to budget your time wisely to convey the most positive image in the time allotted.

If the person setting up the interview is a secretary, you might want to ask if you may call the chair of the committee for more information. When you call the chair, you can explain quite honestly that it is sometimes difficult to hear in a telephone interview. You need not mention that you intend to do some clever detective work beforehand. (You can learn a lot, for example, about the company and it employees on the Internet. Most organizations have Websites and staff directories, so you can clarify job titles. In addition, you can sometimes find a surprising amount of information about committee members' recreational interests and professional affiliations just by Googling names enclosed in quotation marks.)

Because the speakerphone interview is the most difficult, let's assume the worst. If you find yourself participating in a conference call, then so much the better. Either way, you will have only a limited opportunity to react to the committee, so you will want to anticipate their side of the conversation and prepare for it. Remember that phone interviews are more structured than "live and in-person" interviews. Committees want to use their time effectively and still be scrupulously fair to all candidates. They have also discovered that long pauses are more uncomfortable on the telephone.

Interviewing From Home

Telephone interviews tend to be chaotic. You can't hear them; they can't hear you. Be sure that nothing at your end of the line adds to the confusion. This means setting the scene with care. Plan to be at home for the call. You can speak more freely than at work and can better control your environment. If possible, choose a time when other household members are out of the way. Be sure that barking dogs are banished to the backyard. Then decide where you will take the call. Select a desk or table, and a comfortable chair. Place your phone squarely on the table so it does not crash to the floor mid-interview. If your phone is a cordless, be certain that it is fully charged and set up near the base unit for a good, clear connection. Avoid using a cell phone if possible. You never know when the other party will cut out.

Clear the desk or table of everything that does not concern the interview. Having researched the organization, you will want to have this information close at hand during the interview. You will also need pad and pen for taking notes, and a small glass of water is helpful if your voice starts to get froggy. If you're getting over a cold, anticipate a coughing spell with throat lozenges.

Finally, after all your preparation, the telephone rings. A group of people is sitting in a room at the other end of the line. Each one, you must assume, will have a role in the selection decision. You will want to establish a relationship with each. If you were physically present, you would smile, make eye contact, and use gestures to involve them. None of this is possible in a telephone interview. The relationship can only be established through the sound of your voice over the wire.

As each committee member is introduced, repeat the name and title or job responsibility (which you should already have written down in front of you). Then ask a quick question or make a remark that indicates your familiarity with or sympathy for their area of responsibility. Sometimes the chair will simply read the names as part of a prepared introduction and go on to the first question. Establishing rapport with the committee is too important to waste this opportunity. Explain that you want to be sure you heard correctly (use the excuse of the bad connection if necessary), then repeat the names and ask those quick questions. Have additional questions prepared for each person, but don't throw them all at the committee at once. Sprinkle them throughout the conversation and use them to revitalize the discussion when it seems to be dragging. You may not be able to hear the entire response, but try to pick up on a point or two in which you're interested.

Establishing the Right Mood

It is always difficult to know whether you should ask to have comments and questions repeated. Some repetition is necessary or you'll feel as though you're talking to yourself. On the other hand, too much of it can totally destroy the conversation's momentum. You want to maintain an atmosphere conducive to a pleasant, enthusiastic group experience. Your advance preparation will help fit the words you do hear into what you already know, reducing the number of repetitions and allowing you to fill in many of the gaps.

Although it is usually a good rule to let the committee do much of the talking, you may find yourself talking more because you can hear less. It is often the case that the committee can hear you because your voice is being amplified over the speakerphone but not the other way around. Nevertheless, avoid monologues.

The Face-to-Face Interview

Unless there are only a few applicants for a job, the employer must narrow the group from perhaps a dozen potentially acceptable candidates to possibly three or four finalists. When you are called for an interview, it's important to know whether you are one of a larger group or a finalist who will receive more of the interviewer's time and attention. If you are just one of a large group, your work is cut out for you. You will need to make a quick, positive impression. You'll need to make it clear from the start that you are worthy to become a finalist. How do you do this?

Pepping Up Your Image

Younger people sometimes imagine that their elders are all weak and infirm. Just as a child sees everyone past 30 as old, younger employers may look on everyone older than 60 as doddering. Of course, you will project the image of a mature adult, but it must be a healthy, energetic image. Make it obvious to the interviewer that you are physically up to the demands of the job:

- ☞ When you sit down, don't collapse into the chair.

- ☞ When you stand, don't give the impression that it requires a supreme effort to drag yourself up. Many of us have arthritis, and so we may experience some difficulty changing positions. However, unless your condition is severe, you can probably manage to rise from a chair with grace and apparent ease.

- Present a picture of yourself as physically active and interested in new ideas. For example, if you're asked about your hobbies, try to include some that involve physical exertion. Interests that involve considerable interaction with other people are also good to include, but the groups you mention should not include senior citizens.

- Try to get enough sleep the night before the interview and conceal any signs of tiredness. Don't yawn or slump back into the chair.

- Keep your voice crisp and well modulated.

"This is unfair," you may be thinking, as you remember your adolescent grandson who simply melts into any available piece of furniture as if he has no bones at all. Yes, it is unfair, but you are being judged by a different standard. Society assumes that young people have endless energy and older people are on their last gasp. In this guerrilla manual, we deal with the world as it is, not as we would like to have it. Every boomer who triumphs over the job interview, begins a successful second career, and becomes a valued employee will make it just a little easier for the next older applicant.

Anticipating the Interview Questions

Whether you have been invited to an extended interview or brief visit to narrow the competition, "canned" questions tend to be very predictable. If you don't trust your ability to predict them, many books and magazine articles list all the more common ones. Make your own list of potential questions, adding any that you think your resume is likely to generate. Imagine yourself as an interviewer critically scanning your resume. What are the most difficult, most negative questions it might suggest? How can you use those questions as an opportunity or springboard to present positive information about yourself? You might even prepare a written response to each question. Then outline the major points and memorize them. Let me stress the word *written* here. Your answers should be composed when you are feeling relaxed, positive, and upbeat about yourself and your chances of getting the job. The tension of the actual interview may cause you to panic. Without a written outline, your careful preparation could go down the drain.

Researching the Job and the Organization

At least some of the questions will depend on your knowing about the job and the organization. The more you know, the more you can zero in on the employer's needs. That means you'll need to play detective. Before you submitted your application, you did some preliminary research about the organization so you have a head start. Now what else should you know? Examine the job description and announcement. What kind of person are they looking for? Although part of the job ad consists of HR jargon copied word for word from past postings, there will be many small differences that reveal employers' priorities. Of course, they want someone who walks on water, but what does that amount to in real life? There's probably a picture in the back of their minds, and you'll find hints if you look for them. If the job description has been updated recently, it's another good source.

Information about the business or organization can often be found on the World Wide Web. Print out any information you discover and read it carefully. What is its focus? What is its mission? The more you know about the organization, the more you can infer about the job. That can be a big help in an interview. While you're online, do a quick search for the names of the interviewers (enclosed in quotes). If they have been active in professional organizations, you may get some clues to their interests.

The Art of Gentle Redirection

Although you don't want to do all of the talking in an interview, you do want to control it subtly. The larger the group being interviewed, the less time you have to make an impression. In fact, you can be sure of only about half an hour. A good upbeat half hour, however, can be more effective than a long, weary afternoon of cross-examination.

Stay on Message

No matter what the interviewer's questions, you can nearly always manage to get across your most important and positive qualities. Decide what those are in advance. Many of us find it difficult to "sell" ourselves, and we are often more aware of our defects than our assets. A little positive brainstorming, however, will reveal more than enough attractive qualities and areas of expertise to fill the allotted time. Be careful not to go on at length—just a very quick example or two. Time yourself so you take the least amount of time to make the greatest impact. Practice ways to change the subject or revitalize the discussion if it seems to be going downhill. You want it to stay positive, share in your interviewer's enthusiasms, and invite him or her to share in yours. If you must answer a question that reveals a weakness, do it quickly and finish with an upbeat note.

Essential Talking Points

Once you have anticipated as many questions as possible and are ready to make some intelligent responses about the job and the organization, consider what else you would like the interviewer to know. Most interview questions are open-ended, and it is not difficult to segue into your other strengths. Most interviewers are more than willing to let you "do your stuff," because it allows them to see what you are really like. Be sure, however, that you don't appear to be avoiding a question. Answer it fully before you make your segue. Be careful not to talk too much. You don't want to turn your answer into a long monologue, because that is another of the stereotypes about older people. We have all had the experience of struggling to get away from an elderly person who is bent on telling us his or her life story.

Decide What's Important

So what are those strengths you should bring out? First and foremost, you want to make it clear that you have up-to-date skills and an up-to-date attitude. One of the most negative stereotypes about older workers is the belief that they are stuck in a rut and haven't changed with the times. More specifically, they are allergic to computers or have only minimal skills. Without actually bragging, you will want to make it clear that you have been learning and growing. Focus on your recent accomplishments and be sure you can use current computer and occupational jargon effectively. In other words, you want to use the same language as the employer and the more promising applicants.

You're a Proven Commodity

You also want to make it clear that, unlike younger applicants, you are a proven commodity. Be respectful but identify with the perspective of the interviewer. You understand what it's like to hold a demanding job and you can see the selection process from the employer's side of the table. You have "been there, done that," but be careful. If you overdo it and turn your responses into long laundry lists of jobs you've held, you will ruin your chances. Mention your earlier experience only in a general way and focus on accomplishments and transferable skills, not job titles.

Making the Interview Enjoyable

Whether you are participating in a face-to-face or telephone interview, it's a good idea to assume that interviewers may be tired and, mere mortals that they are, can quickly become bored. One applicant may begin to look and sound like another. They have difficulty sorting out who said what, and names and faces become jumbled together. Make the session as enjoyable as possible. As you prepare, don't neglect humorous stories that illustrate your points. Everyone likes to be told a story, but they shouldn't be long ones. Interviewers may encourage you to talk but they will be more alert while they themselves are doing the talking. Keep asking questions throughout the interview. Interviewers usually have a formal list of questions, so responses will tend to be similar. Try to make yours memorable.

Fine-Tuning Your Image

Although the image you project in an interview is undoubtedly you, it is just a very quick snapshot. When you don't get a job after an interview, you may imagine the interviewer as a judge standing in judgment and finding you guilty. Always remember that these are people who really know very little about you. They didn't reject you. The "you" that was communicated in the interview was only a brief glimpse. You can learn something new from each interview and incorporate what you learn into the next one. With careful planning, that brief ordeal can become both an accurate reflection of you and your many assets and an effective vehicle for winning the job you want.

After the Interview

You've decided that your next job will be different from all the others. It will provide opportunities for you to express yourself more fully and use your talents in more creative and satisfying ways. With this goal in mind, you have prepared yourself for today's job market, identified an opening that interests you, and earned an interview. The big question now is not really if you will get the job. Of course, that is important, but there is an even bigger question: Is this really the job you thought it was?

Would this job give you the opportunity to make the changes in your life that you're planning? You've met some of the people with whom you would be working. Although they were probably on their best behavior, you probably got a feeling for the kind of atmosphere they have created. How did it feel? Did you sense a feeling of camaraderie? Did the boss and his or her subordinates seem to be comfortable with one another? Did they laugh and joke together or was there a more formal and possibly strained relationship? Of course, there's no way to know for sure, but you've worked at a lot of different jobs. You can look back and remember the atmosphere that was typical of a happy, productive workplace.

Should You Take the Job?

In the past, you probably assumed that you'd take a job if it were offered. Just as long as the salary and benefits met your requirements and there did not seem to be any obvious drawbacks, you grasped that next rung on the ladder. Think back to the last time you were offered a new job. After leaping up every time you heard the phone ring and awaiting each mail delivery, the magic moment arrived. You were somehow informed that you were selected for the position. Probably, you kept your cool during the brief conversation but danced a joyous jig after you put the phone back on its cradle. Did you accept the job? Of course you did, or maybe you gave yourself a day or so to think about it.

You Make the Choice

This time, however, it's just as important for you to choose the job as it is to be the one chosen. Old habits die hard, and the excitement of a job offer can pull you along, preventing you from ever making a real decision. An acquaintance I'll call Barbara was telling me about her new job. About six months ago, she decided to change her life. She decided that she was going to spend more time developing her talents and interests. Her job did not allow her to move in this direction, so Barbara decided that she would find one that really met her needs. Quick as a flash, she began looking for job openings.

Over the years Barbara had become so good at investigating employers and putting application packages together that you might say she went into autopilot. In fact, she was so skilled and so efficient at job-hunting that, within a few months, she actually had a job offer. How exciting it was to get that telephone call! How joyously she celebrated her success! Barbara had been in her new job for a few months when I last talked with her. It was, she said, very much like her old job.

She'd gotten the job because she was so well qualified. She'd done it all before. Wasn't that the very problem she started out with? Of course, her ego is in better shape because she knows she still has what it takes. That kind of affirmation is important when you're in your 50s or 60s. Barbara is enjoying the change of scene but essentially her life hasn't changed. Within a few months, she'll probably be just as discontent as she was in the old job. And what about all those skills and talents she was going to develop? The new job only uses the old Barbara's skills.

The Rest of the Plan

Remember that, although money is a consideration, the job is just one part of your overall plan for a better life. Before you began job-hunting, you took a long, honest look at the ways in which you wanted to change your life. You examined the jobs you held during your career, listing what you liked and what you disliked about each. You also looked at the life you were leading and compared it to the kind of life you wanted to lead. You considered your hobbies and other leisure activities, and your family and friends. It's time to find those lists and revisit the conclusions you reached.

If the new job does not meet the needs of the person you have become, then you probably should not take it. When you go through your list point by point, do you feel confident of a good fit? If not, force yourself back to the real world. Get your ego under control and don't allow the "thrill of the chase" to mislead you. If, however, you believe this job really is different and will bring out your strengths, then a wonderful opportunity awaits you. Have some fun, and celebrate with champagne if you like, but remember that you still have some work ahead.

12 Surviving and Thriving After Probation

Now that you've gotten the job, you might think the rest is "duck soup." You've achieved your goal and now you can sit back and enjoy your triumph. Not so. That may have been how you reacted when you were offered your last job or the one before, but this one is different. Remember that your goal is not just to get a job but to enjoy it, to live a more rewarding, satisfying life. If your life is going to be different, then this job must be different as well.

Your first hurdle will be to survive the probationary period. Most employers designate a period of time during which you are, in a sense, on trial. Even if your employer has no official probationary period, this is nevertheless the time when you and your work will be closely examined. If you survive and receive a favorable evaluation, you usually become a permanent employee with some measure of job security.

Leave Your Baggage Behind

Probation is a time when you become adjusted to the job. You learn what is expected of you, develop relationships with bosses and coworkers, and gradually find your way around the work environment. This should also be the time when you adjust your mental attitude toward your work. If you look back into your past, you'll probably remember that, after a while, new jobs came to resemble the ones you left behind. You were the same person with the same skills, goals, and attitudes. Of course, there were more satisfying jobs and more stressful jobs but, in general, you tended to approach your work and your coworkers in the same way. This wasn't necessarily a bad thing, but it is not how you want to approach this new job. There is an overused cliché about today being the first day of the rest of your life. Clichéd or not, that is a good way to approach this period of adjustment.

Although money can't be ignored, it is not really the reason you took this job. If it were, you would probably have stayed on in your old job. No, this is the job you plan to enjoy. You plan to come to work each day looking forward to seeing friends, learning new things, and expanding your horizons. It is unlikely that those were your goals the last time you began a new job. To put it in a nutshell, your goal was probably advancement (defined as frequent pay raises and promotions). Advancement meant perks such as a large office or acceptance into the upper echelon of management. If consciously or unconsciously you bring those goals to this new job, you can't expect to get out of your rut. This job will soon become the same as all the others that came before it.

To put it another way, this should be a time when you cast off the baggage you've been carrying around from those past jobs. Sometimes work can bring out the worst in you. For example, competition may have made you a little paranoid about your coworkers. You may never have felt the pleasure of really being part of a team and there was always a little distrust that spoiled the camaraderie. Now, you plan to enjoy the pleasure of being with other people and making lasting friendships, but that won't happen if you bring that old paranoia with you.

The Case of Catherine

Catherine's story may give you an idea of what can go wrong if you bring those old habits with you to the new job. Catherine was 58 and clearly the best-qualified applicant for the job. The manager who hired her had some reservations during the interview. Catherine did most of the talking.

Although it's important to communicate your strengths in an interview, Catherine overdid it. Over the years, she had worked at a variety of jobs and acquired many skills. The problem was she couldn't help bragging about them.

Interviewers expect applicants to sell themselves, so this didn't bother the interviewer too much. However, she also noticed that Catherine didn't really seem to be listening when she described the job. Nevertheless, it was clear that Catherine had better experience and stronger educational qualifications than the other applicants. Reluctantly, she decided to offer Catherine the job.

Unfortunately, Catherine's interview was a pretty accurate preview of her on-the-job behavior. She knew how the job should be done because she'd done it all before. Because she was usually thinking about what she would say next, she did not notice that her boss had a different view of the job. Catherine worked hard, just as she always had. She sometimes worked through her lunch hour and, of course, she couldn't help telling everyone what a mess her department was in. Unfortunately, it didn't occur to Catherine that she was not making progress on the projects she'd been assigned. Once again, she wasn't really listening. She had just transferred her old job description and her old habits to the new assignment.

Catherine's boss was at first impressed with her diligence. Unlike the Generation X-ers around her, she rarely goofed off. However, whenever they met to discuss Catherine's work, they never seemed to get around to the assigned projects. Instead, Catherine talked nonstop about all her other superior accomplishments. Catherine assumed that, when the boss saw how much she'd done, she would understand that Catherine knew best.

When deadlines approached, however, it became clear that Catherine was not going to meet them. Gradually, the boss's attitude changed. She felt as if she were talking to a stone wall. Nothing she said seemed to make any impression.

Catherine never really listened to her boss. The work-place had been changing, and that meant that new strate-gies to deal with change had become necessary as well. If Catherine had been willing to listen, she could have gotten cues from her boss and her coworkers. Younger people have grown up in a very different world, and these differences are reflected in the way they approach their work. Catherine could have become more sensitive to differences in outlook and philosophy that characterize generations. Today's work environment is in some ways a foreign country for many boomers and seniors. They don't understand the language or the customs. To fit in, they must keep their eyes and ears open to pick up clues. Just as they cannot remain out-siders and function effectively in a foreign country, they can't be outsiders at work, oblivious of all that surrounds them.

One of the big changes in recent years has been the in-creasing importance of teams and teamwork. Catherine had always been a lone wolf. She was highly competitive and, at work, competition always won out over collaboration. As younger employees with different interests and work habits gradually replaced the old guard, she felt isolated. At her last job, her coworkers grew tired of hearing about her ac-complishments and nicknamed her "Ms. Know-it-All."

Now in her wonderful new job, she made no effort to be part of the team. She was unwilling to go to her coworkers for help, as that was an admission of weakness. If she had made an effort to speak their language and accept their guid-ance, everything might have turned out okay. Instead, she wanted to tell them how everything should be done.

When a group really becomes a team, something special happens. They gradually come to share a vision; they de-velop a more creative, more effective way of approaching their work. The group develops a synergy, and together they can sometimes come up with much better ideas than indi-viduals working separately. Coworkers at first tried to bring

Catherine into the group, but when she rejected their attempts, they turned against her. When they saw that she was in trouble, they felt no obligation to support her.

There was another problem with Catherine's work: she had oversold herself. Because she had purchased a home computer, surfed the Web occasionally, and corresponded with her children by e-mail, she touted her computer literacy. In fact, she claimed much better computer skills than she possessed. It had never occurred to her to take a computer course or attend a workshop, because she didn't really believe that computers were important. Catherine had managed to do her work efficiently for years without the help of a computer and she saw no reason why she couldn't continue that way.

Computers aren't a minor change in the work environment; they have revolutionized it. Most jobs have been completely changed by computers. Employees who are really computer-literate understand what a computer can do and what it can't do. They have integrated computers into their work and use them as they would extra arms or legs. To Catherine, the computer was a toy, not really essential to her work. When the group used computer terms, she didn't know what they meant. Gradually she became defensive, realizing that she would have to fake computer savvy. That was part of the reason she hadn't completed her assigned projects. She understood very little of the orientation she received from the in-house technician and was unwilling to reveal her ignorance. Now she needed to obtain data and produce statistical tables that required sophisticated computer skills.

Finally, it never occurred to Catherine that her boss was a real person, who might be experiencing discomfort supervising someone old enough to be her mother. It never occurred to her that the boss needed to feel that she, not Catherine, was in control. However, Catherine was far from stupid. She could see that even though she herself had more experience, she had to appear appropriately humble and cooperative. In fact, she continually said, "You're the boss" and "I'm happy to do it your way," although this was merely lip service. Though she appeared to be accepting the boss's authority, she really did as she thought best.

Gradually her boss realized that Catherine was out of control. She found herself caught between the demands of senior managers on the one side, and Catherine's mistaken priorities on the other. When she was at last fired, Catherine considered suing her employer for age discrimination. Had she chosen this route, she might have had a pretty good case. Her young boss, new to the manager's role, had failed to establish the careful paper trail recommended by human resource professionals. She had been impressed by Catherine's self-confidence and knowledge, and she continued to think that, if Catherine could only be made to understand what was expected of her, all would be well. Hence, her boss failed to make it clear to Catherine that she was in danger of losing her job.

Fortunately, Catherine's lawyer was honest with her. Yes, she might win a discrimination suit, but it probably wouldn't be worth the effort. Not only would legal fees make a large dent in any financial settlement she received, but the case would probably take a year or more out of her life. During that year, she would have to relive the experience over and over. Financial settlements are rarely large enough to repay anyone for the stress and mental turmoil. About all Catherine was likely to get out of a discrimination suit was revenge. After talking with her lawyer, she chose to get on with her life.

In a nutshell, here's what went wrong. Catherine was the new kid in the office. Despite her long experience, she was a novice at this particular job. Yes, her past experience would be useful. Yes, she had done similar work before. However, she failed to realize that this was a completely new job with new demands and expectations. Catherine's most important priority was to learn—to be open to her new environment, to understand the language of her coworkers, and to become part of the culture that was shared by this particular group of people. Instead of helping her, Catherine's past experience actually hurt her chances of success. It got in the way of her seeing her new job clearly, and it kept her from listening, really listening, to the advice and instruction she received. Then, too, her inflated ego prevented her from accepting help from her coworkers. Jockeying for a place in the organizational hierarchy, she saw them as competitors rather than teammates.

Had she made some attitude adjustments, Catherine probably could have been successful. Her boss was appreciative of her talents and willing to work with her. This is not always the case. Occasionally, a senior employee encounters a boss who is too inflexible to tolerate individual differences. Perhaps Tom's story can illustrate this kind of situation.

The Case of Tom

Tom was an extrovert and found retirement a bore. It simply didn't provide the social stimulation he had found in his former career. Yet he knew he couldn't go back to the old rat race. After taking a good look at himself and what he really wanted to get out of his work, Tom applied for a job in a call center of a well-known computer service provider. The job, he reasoned, would allow him to use his computer skills, and he could spend his time on the telephone with people who needed his help.

Although Tom was sometimes chided for spending too much time with individual callers, he found the job suited him. It satisfied his social needs, and he felt he was doing something useful. However, he was well aware that call-center jobs are poorly paid and low in status. Although he was not really unhappy with the job, he was not accustomed to being what he called a "grunt."

Within his organization, those who trained new employees were given a higher status than those who merely answered the phones. Wouldn't it be a good idea to continue enjoying people and computers but gain a little respect? Tom decided to seek a promotion. Because his record was good and he had done a little teaching, he was promoted to trainer when the next opening occurred.

At the interview, Tom's new boss, Paul, came across as someone he'd enjoy working for. He spoke enthusiastically about creative teaching techniques and seemed open to new ideas. Tom looked forward to his first day of work in such a stimulating environment.

At first, the new job seemed to be all he'd hoped it would be. After the first week, Tom realized that he had exactly the talents and experience needed to be a successful trainer. He got along well with his students and found that his teaching skills were well suited to the job. Unlike Catherine, Tom understood that he was the new kid on the block and sought out Paul's help on many occasions. He listened carefully, asked questions, and took many of Paul's suggestions to heart. As time went on, however, he began to feel more confident. He incorporated ideas not only from Paul, but also from his past experience, his new coworkers, and his reading, ultimately developing a style that worked for him. In the eyes of his students and his peers, Tom was a successful trainer.

Unfortunately, this opinion was not shared by his supervisor. Each time he met with Paul, he received thinly veiled criticism. Why hadn't he done this or that? Paul never actually said that he was doing a bad job; yet he never seemed satisfied. Although Tom's students went on to become productive employees, his relationship with Paul went steadily downhill. What made the situation especially painful was that Tom was gradually losing his confidence. He was wondering if he really knew how to do the job or if he was just an old dog who could no longer learn new tricks.

In our earlier example, Catherine was too inflexible to adapt to her new work environment. Younger people, however, can be just as inflexible as their elders, especially when they lack the self-confidence to tolerate new ideas. The other trainers Paul hired lacked experience. They were young people, promoted from the call-center phone pool, who came with no previous knowledge of the field. Paul could indoctrinate them with all his personal techniques, opinions, and prejudices. In a sense, they were clay ready to be molded into "Paul clones." However, there was no way that Tom could become Paul's clone. He was a fully developed, mature individual who couldn't help but bring his own personality and experience to the job. Despite his professed openness to new ideas, Paul was unable to see that another approach could be as successful as his own. Not only was his perspective a narrow one, but he felt threatened by an employee who exhibited any independence.

Tom found himself sleeping badly, neglecting the hobbies he enjoyed, and dreading each workday. Finally, a friend confronted him. Wasn't the reason he changed to a new career track to have fun? Wasn't the new job supposed to be less stressful than the old one? Why was Tom taking a very large pay cut to do something that made him lose sleep at night?

When it was put to him that way, Tom's course was clear. The next day, he stopped in to see his old boss in the call center and asked if he could have his job back.

Is This What You Wanted?

Your new boss is not the only one who should be evaluating you during the probationary period. You should be taking a good look at yourself and the way you are feeling about the new job. Don't let too much time pass before you step back and take an honest look at how things are going. Here are some questions that may help you get started:

↠ **Are you having fun?**

This is perhaps the first and most important question that
you should ask yourself. If you're not enjoying your time
at work, then you haven't achieved your goal. If you're
not quite sure of your answer, try to pin down the reason
why you're uneasy. Of course, it's natural to be nervous
when you're dealing with a lot of new people and new
information. Once things begin to settle down, however,
you will want to start "smelling the roses." If you're not
finding this job more fun than your last one, could it be
that you're not looking for fun? Have you brought with
you all those negative attitudes that built up over the
course of your last job?

↠ **Are you having trouble catching on?**

Are you feeling stressed by all the new things that you're
learning? Sometimes we become a little frightened or anx-
ious when it seems as if we aren't learning the ropes as
quickly as we used to. It's true that our brains are not as
quick as they were when we were younger, although
they're just as serviceable. Take a lot of notes when things
are explained to you. After you have met with your supervisor, go back to your desk, look over your notes, and
write or type out everything you can remember from the
meeting. Just the act of taking the notes and going over
them will embed them in your memory. Keep your notes
in a well-organized notebook and read them over from
time to time.

   Successful boomers say that an important key to aging gracefully and productively is knowing themselves,
and being honest about their physical and mental limitations. They know, for example, that their short-term
memories are becoming somewhat unreliable, but that
doesn't mean they're any less intelligent or competent.
One 70-something executive says she never goes anywhere
without a notepad. She uses Microsoft Outlook as an alarm
clock, entering the date and time of every appointment

and setting an alarm to go off 15 minutes before it is scheduled to begin. She also carries a small date book. That way she can make note of every meeting as it is scheduled and then transfer the information to her Outlook program. It's a little more work, but the routine has become almost automatic. Because she is forced to copy the information concerning her appointments, she is more likely to remember it.

❧ Are you feeling critical of your boss or your colleagues?

Sometimes we criticize others to avoid accepting our own limitations. Do you find yourself complaining that younger colleagues don't speak up; they just mumble? Maybe you need a hearing aid. When a problem arises, deal with it. Don't look for someone else to blame.

❧ When you talk with younger staff, are you using the tone you use with your own children?

If you can't treat your coworkers as grown-ups, how can you expect them to include you? When we complain about prejudice, we tend to forget that we are often guilty of this kind of reverse ageism.

❧ Do you find yourself avoiding your computer?

Did you bypass the computer chapter in this book (Chapter 9)? If so, it's time for you to go back to it. You will probably learn computer skills more quickly if you purchase your own home computer. Then you can spend some time with it in the evenings doing things that you find enjoyable. As computers become standard issue for all or most employees, there is no way you can avoid them and be a successful employee.

❧ Is your computer screen hard to read?

It doesn't have to be. There are a dozen or more adjustments that might increase your comfort level. Windows XP and Vista have both an Accessibility Wizard and a brief course to help you use it more effectively.

Word-processing text, desktop program icons, and your mouse pointer can all be enlarged, and mouse buttons can be reversed if they are uncomfortable for you. The magnifier can enlarge specific parts of the screen that are especially hard to read, and a high-contrast color scheme can also make it easier to read the text.

➴ **Have you met at least one person who is likely to become a good friend?**

It's the friendships we make at work that give us the most pleasure. Make it a point to have lunch and coffee breaks with your coworkers. Even though you may feel tempted to work through break periods, the pleasure of being with friends is one of the most important reasons why many people choose to work past retirement age.

Putting It All Together

Now that we boomers have arrived at the ripe old age of 50 or 60, it's time to take a good look at who we are and what we want out of life. We're grown-ups now (although we sometimes feel like silly teenagers). All those years of experience that we have under our belts are a treasure trove. We really do know things that we didn't know when we were 20 or 30, and we want to put them to use. Space shuttle crews talk of making mid-course corrections, and it's time we made our own mid-course corrections. Fortunately, modern medicine has given us enough years to not only change our direction, but enjoy our destination when we get there.

Index

About the Author

JEANNETTE WOODWARD is a founder and principal of the Wind River Nonprofit and Educational Consulting Group. Before becoming a consultant, Woodward was a library manager with many years' experience as both an interviewer and a job hunter. Her books include *Nonprofit Essentials: Managing Technology* (John Wiley & Sons, 2006), *Creating the Customer-Driven Library* (American Library Association, 2004), and the college writing textbook *Writing Research Papers: Investigating Resources in Cyberspace* (McGraw-Hill, 1999). Woodward holds a masters degree and has worked toward a doctorate at the University of Texas. She lives in Lander, Wyoming, in the foothills of the Rockies.